TEACHING SOCIAL SKILLS THROUGH SKETCH COMEDY AND IMPROV GAMES

of related interest

Social Skills Games for Children
Deborah M. Plummer
ISBN 978 1 84310 617 3
ISBN 978 1 84985 589 1 (Large Print)
eISBN 978 1 84642 836 4

Social Skills, Emotional Growth and Drama Therapy
Inspiring Connection on the Autism Spectrum
Lee R. Chasen
ISBN 978 1 84905 840 7
eISBN 978 0 85700 345 4

Acting Antics
A Theatrical Approach to Teaching Social Understanding
to Kids and Teens with Asperger Syndrome
Cindy B. Schneider
ISBN 978 1 84310 845 0
eISBN 978 1 84642 589 9

Sandtray Play and Storymaking
A Hands-On Approach to Build Academic, Social, and
Emotional Skills in Mainstream and Special Education
Sheila Dorothy Smith
ISBN 978 1 84905 205 4
eISBN 978 0 85700 436 9

Outsmarting Worry
An Older Kid's Guide to Managing Anxiety
Dawn Huebner PhD
Illustrated by Kara McHale
ISBN 978 1 78592 782 9
eISBN 978 1 78450 702 2

TEACHING SOCIAL SKILLS THROUGH SKETCH COMEDY AND IMPROV GAMES

A Social Theatre™ Approach for Kids and Teens including those with ASD, ADHD, and Anxiety

SHAWN AMADOR

Jessica Kingsley *Publishers*
London and Philadelphia

First published in 2018
by Jessica Kingsley Publishers
73 Collier Street
London N1 9BE, UK
and
400 Market Street, Suite 400
Philadelphia, PA 19106, USA

www.jkp.com

Library of Congress Cataloging in Publication Data
A CIP catalog record for this book is available from the Library of Congress

British Library Cataloguing in Publication Data
A CIP catalogue record for this book is available from the British Library

ISBN 978 1 78592 800 0
eISBN 978 1 78450 820 3

Printed and bound by CPI Group (UK) Ltd, Croydon, CR0 4YY

CONTENTS

BREAKDOWN CHART BY SOCIAL THINKING® PROFILE LEVEL AND TARGET SKILLS

Activities	Social Level			Skills						
	Challenged	Emerging	Nuance	Eye Contact	Joint Focus	Recognizing Social Cues	Perspective Taking	Collaborative Imagination	Feelings Recognition	Flexibility
Scarf Juggling	Challenged Social Communicator	Emerging Social Communicator	Nuance Challenged Social Communicator	✓	✓	✓		✓		
Blanket Folding				✓	✓	✓		✓	✓	✓
Mirroring				✓	✓	✓	✓	✓	✓	✓
Playing Boo				✓	✓	✓		✓		
Voice Levels					✓	✓			✓	
Feeling or Action?					✓	✓			✓	
Levels of Emotions					✓	✓			✓	
Feelings Charades				✓	✓	✓	✓		✓	
Slow Motion Snowball Fight				✓	✓	✓		✓		✓
Room Chi				✓	✓	✓			✓	✓
Dance Party				✓	✓	✓		✓		✓

Activities	Social Level			Skills						
	Challenged	Emerging	Nuance	Eye Contact	Joint Focus	Recognizing Social Cues	Perspective Taking	Collaborative Imagination	Feelings Recognition	Flexibility
The Puppeteer Improv Game				✓	✓	✓	✓	✓	✓	✓
Using Stage Levels	Challenged Social Communicator	Emerging Social Communicator	Nuance Challenged Social Communicator	✓	✓	✓		✓		✓
Conversational Reciprocity Improv Game				✓	✓	✓		✓		✓
Practicing and Understanding "Awkward"				✓	✓	✓	✓			✓
Foundation Improv Activity					✓	✓	✓	✓		✓
Assertive Training Cards Appendix C				✓	✓	✓			✓	
Using Magic to Teach Perspective Taking				✓	✓	✓	✓	✓		✓

When acting, the rule of thumb is that one is practicing all of the skills listed above. To add more perspective taking, have participants switch roles often. To add more specified skills during skits, remind participants what they are working on.

Source: Author

PREFACE

Since I began working with children and youth as a school social worker, I always sought out different ways and opportunities to increase their self-esteem and to have their voices heard. It was always my intention to gather the plays that had been written from my afterschool sketch comedy program and publish them in a playbook. Parents and their children alike have been excited about the possibility and have been supportive—giving permission to utilize the ideas and collaboratively written plays. Publishing the plays was a way to help those I worked with to feel that they have a voice and to know that the topics and lessons they wrote about are truly important.

As I continued with the afterschool program, I began to realize the power of script-writing, practicing, and performing. It was easy to see how it provided not only a humorous outlet, but behavioral rehearsal of effective and ineffective solutions, as well as the opportunity for kids to come up with their own effective solutions. Therefore, I decided to carry out an ethnographic study of the program while in graduate school. With the parents' permission, I interviewed participants, who identified the strengths of the program. When analyzing the scripts and idea files, I found there was a script-writing process. While continuing to establish my program, I also utilized theatre in different settings with adults and children who had differences such as cognitive disabilities and autism. I found that even with those who had significant disabilities, improv theatre could be modified for these populations.

Through incorporating and modifying improv in different settings and with differing abilities, I have found a way to modify improv to different levels of abilities as well as helping participants through collaborative playwriting. In collaborative playwriting,

I have developed different steps and lessons in order to guide the process. Looking at how to develop a basic afterschool program into a program with deeper, more clinical strategies has taken a lot of creativity and time. Even though the initial goal was to publish student plays only, I have found a deeper focus within the program. Main themes within the program include how to break down improv to teach social-cognitive skills by level and to teach social skills through the collaborative process of script-writing. With my explorations of utilizing theatrical strategies along with the playwriting process, I have found it is much more helpful to teach social emotional concepts before a play is rehearsed, in order to help build more participant knowledge of the focus of the plays. It is important for participants to understand the social emotional concepts, not only for themselves, but also because they will be teaching the concepts to others during their performance.

ACKNOWLEDGEMENTS

First of all, to my students and other Social Theatre™ participants: *you* are *amazing* and wonderful. I am incredibly proud of each and every one of you. I hope you find that after all your hard work in collaborating with each other and seeing the skits in writing that this is empowering for you! You have all been through this process of playwriting, accepting each other's ideas, into performance, and now a published book. Each and every one of you is talented and can do so much in this world!

To the administrators at my schools, board members, parents, community members, and colleagues at CORE Connection: thank you for your belief in my wacky ideas, and for supporting me for all of these years. It is because of your support that I could help the children at our schools and community through embracing creative minds. To Patch Adams, for taking the time to speak with me, for supplying my students with the amazing materials, including the *Clown in Kabul* CD and the book *House Calls* which also helped guide some of my lessons in teaching in classrooms as well. Moreover, I really appreciate your guidance in pointing me in the right direction of research and your encouragement of my clown program.

To my husband and children: thank you for understanding my fatigue and need to sleep during the time I endured late hours to write this book! I love you very much!

To my parents and brother: thank you for always believing in me, no matter what.

Chapter One

HISTORY OF SOCIAL THEATRE™

Growing up, I attended a music, arts, and drama camp every summer, where I learned about clowning. From this experience, I recognized the value in having an accepting environment where kids of any age could use their imagination and play together. Furthermore, I also know that when our clients and students think of social learning, they do not equate the idea with fun. However, when using Social Theatre™ groups, participants do not feel as if they are learning. In fact, performing about social mistakes and having opportunities to correct the social situations for a better, more effective choice, actually appears more like sketch comedy!

The origins of Social Theatre™ began in 2000 as an afterschool clown troupe program which morphed into a Comedy Improv Troupe in a regular education school on the southwest side of Chicago. Then, the program transitioned into a sketch comedy improv troupe called "Social Theatre." Moreover, I have also begun a "Social Theatre™" group therapy program in a clinic where the focus is working with children with anxiety and social deficits while utilizing the program on a deeper level.

Throughout the development of my program, I have maintained knowledge of trending research in the field of social skills development through theatre programs. In consideration of the need for research-based programs, I strived to ensure our methodology followed those shown to be most effective by current research. In light of the fact I had my own evolving program, I wanted to learn more about the roots of my program and participant viewpoints. Therefore, in 2009, having parental and school permission to conduct an ethnographic study, I was able to study my original clown program to analyze more of its components, as well as what it meant to the participants. Participants described the clown program as having components of "stress relief," "humor," "teamwork," and "role modeling." Moreover, in the ethnographic study, participants described the program as enabling them to "teach what we learn." Although our clown program has morphed into sketch comedy, it has the same mission and purpose, namely, to actively learn social skills and then teach the skills to others.

In analyzing written ideas, notes, and plays, I looked at five years of all of the paper notes the afterschool troupe had brainstormed and written. Through the script analysis component of the ethnographic study, I discovered that we had a script development process. Then, I grouped different stages of writings, which formed the foundations of our collaborative writing process. These foundations we found were made up of brainstorming single-word ideas, phrases with one or two details, more developed ideas with collaboration, and final scripts. Over the years, we have developed our collaborative writing process by utilizing the foundational information from the ethnographic study, along with what has worked in our group experience. The steps include: (1) brainstorming rules; (2) brainstorming; (3) preparation for evaluating; (4) grouping ideas from brainstorms; (5) validating each other's ideas while evaluating, and re-writing; and (6) role assignment.

As we have solidified our script development process, we have been able to establish specific activities that fall under teamwork and collaboration, as well as stress relief. Moreover, we also utilize specific social emotional concepts as part of teaching social emotional skills in our plays.

SOCIAL THEATRE™ IN CLASSROOMS, AFTERSCHOOL PROGRAMS, AND THERAPEUTIC ENVIRONMENTS

Presently, I utilize strategies from Social Theatre™ throughout the school day within the school as well as conducting small therapy groups using Social Theatre™. During the school day, I have co-led small classroom groups during a language arts class to teach collaborative skills through group writing. Moreover, we have held school-wide playwriting contests, which feeds back into the collaborative process described in Chapter Three. In addition participants from the afterschool program often help teach concepts in classes through performing skits or improv activities. When working with individual clients, I have also used the script-writing process and they are invited to share their script by bringing it to our afterschool program.

Due to decreasing levels of face-to-face interaction in everyday life, interactive social skills programs are increasingly needed. These programs are essential in boosting confidence while providing opportunities to enhance interpersonal communications. Research shows that theatre and improvisation can help bridge this gap. Specifically, studies show that collaboration, improvisation, and theatre are effective in increasing social skills, imagination, coping skills, and academic skills.

RESEARCH-BASED PRACTICE

Two studies by Corbett *et al.* (2014a, b) measured outcomes in a camp model lasting 10 days of 3½ hours and a 2½-month theatre program of approximately 40 hours. SENSE Theatre stands for "Social Emotional NeuroScience Endocrinology Theatre" and was developed by Blythe Corbett, a professor and researcher at Vanderbilt University. In the SENSE Theatre program, youth aged 7–18 who were on the autism spectrum were paired with trained peer models during theatre classes. The outcomes included significantly decreased anxiety, increased theory of mind skills, and increased interaction during unstructured time with peers. More specifically, participant stress levels were measured through a saliva cortisol sample, which showed significant decrease of stress over the two weeks of theatre camp (Corbett *et al.* 2014a). Corbett *et al.*'s studies (2011, 2014b) further supported theatre interventions to increase social, adaptive, and perspective taking skills. Guli *et al.* (2013) measured qualitative and quantitative results of an improvisational theatre intervention experimental group compared to a traditional group of participants with autism spectrum disorder and attention deficit hyperactivity disorder (ADHD). The research studied the "Social Competence Intervention Program" alongside a control group for 8–12 weeks, which included a total of 24 hours of training. The Social Competence Intervention Program included improvisation games with the goal of teaching social skills such as inferencing, feelings recognition, perception, social attention, and group cohesion, among others. Through qualitative measures of client and parent report, 75 percent of parents reported improvement and 82 percent of clients reported improvement. A computerized, visual test (Diagnostic Analysis of Nonverbal Accuracy, or DANVA2) indicated that the experimental group showed an increase in the area of understanding social cues compared to the control group. Participants were observed within their school environment to examine possible generalization of skills; the statistical results showed an improvement for the experimental group in the areas of understanding social cues, a decrease in solitary play, and an increase in peer interaction.

In a study by DeMichele (2015), a dramatic increase in writing was shown when improvisational theatre was incorporated into language arts classes. The control group consisting of a traditional language arts class showed a 78 percent increase in student writing, while the experimental group with improvisational theatre interventions in a language arts class showed a 209 percent increase in student writing. For students with cognitive disabilities and learning differences, the increase was even more dramatic. The students with cognitive disabilities and learning differences showed a 49 percent increase in their writings in the traditional language arts class versus those with cognitive disabilities and learning differences in the improvisational theatre-based language arts class, who increased their writings by 309 percent. DeMichele stresses the importance of building trust by creating a non-judgmental, accepting environment, and building ideas through improvisational theatre work in the classroom, which allows increased idea flow.

Agnihotri and colleagues' (2012) case study of a theatre and arts program, which worked with participants with brain disorders, reported increased time with peers, increased social perspective skills, and decreased stress levels among participants. In my own work, I have found that a program utilizing arts-based modalities such as writing, sketch comedy, and improvisational theatre, allows participants to find stress relief through humor and the ability to laugh together about social awkwardness, yet at the same time learning how to be social.

Related results taken from a study by Seih et al. (2011) found that writing in the first person was shown to increase perspective taking. When acting a certain part, I have also found that participants increase their ability to see another perspective. In fact, when someone is having difficulty seeing a certain type of perspective, I challenge that participant to try out a similar role.

Those with social deficits often have difficulty with interrupting or with others interrupting them, and it is often difficult for them to understand when interrupting is and is not appropriate. Vass *et al.* (2008) concluded in a study that collaborative writing has its own process and expectations. During the brainstorming process, interrupting and overlapping is typical as participants become excited about others' ideas. They might complete each other's sentences, talk in short phrases, or even interrupt as they build off each other's ideas. In collaborative writing, the process of brainstorming is essential.

I've also found that, when brainstorming, participants will blurt out ideas that pertain to personal aspects of their lives. Oftentimes, these details had not been brought up in therapy or discussions with parents or teachers. Bereiter and Scardamalia (1987) conducted a study in which they found that brainstorming is very similar to free association.

Various coping skills were assessed for effectiveness within a diverse, urban youth population in a study by Vera *et al.* (2012). Out of all of the types of coping skills, Vera *et al.* found that humor was the greatest buffer between stress and negative affect.

A common difficulty for participants who do group work is letting go of their original ideas or allowing changes to be made to their script. I find this is hard for students who participate in classroom group work, as well as for children participating in pretend play. In theatre and in collaborative writing, the process of brainstorming, writing, and making revisions can be taught. Centerstage's *Teaching Playwriting in Schools: Teacher's Handbook* (n.d.) discusses that participants might initially have difficulty when asked to revise parts, but are much more accepting of the revision process when they see the finished product. Also important is that humor is a way to help relieve stress. Many studies discuss the benefits of humor to health (Berk, L.S. *et al.* 1989; Kamei, T. and Hiroaki, K. 1997) and psychological well-being (Kuiper, N.A. *et al.* 1983; Vera *et al.* 2012). One can only imagine how creating positive humor together can foster more happiness, more positivity, less stress, and greater relationships. Patch Adams, the infamous doctor clown, utilizes humor as a basis for caregiving in his own practice as well as at the Gesundheit Hospital and Clinic. In his book *Gesundheit* (1998), Patch discusses the positive brain chemistry and body effects that contribute to physical and emotional well-being. In his book *House Calls* (1998), Patch discusses the importance of the imagination and creativity in living a full and happy life.

To summarize, decreased stress levels (Agnihotri *et al.* 2012; Corbett *et al.* 2014a, b), increased idea flow (DeMichele 2015), and perspective taking (Agnihotri *et al.* 2012; Corbett *et al.* 2014a, b) are all benefits of participation in improvisational theatre. In collaborative writing, participants learn how to share and accept ideas as well as how to work in a group. In Social Theatre™, participants learn how to collaborate as they utilize improvisation and brainstorming in the process of playwriting. Participants work with each other to develop an end product all members can feel good about. After practicing the social skills that they write about, participants go into the community to teach others about social skills through their skits. This allows the participants to feel a greater sense of pride, as they are able to teach what they have learned and created.

This book describes the process of Social Theatre™ and its components, which include a collaborative writing process, improvisational activities, and skits. Since 2000, when I first started running the Sahs Comedy Improv Troupe and more recent theatre modality in my private practice, I have developed this program alongside my students and clients. Although we have always written scripts about social issues and social skills, recently we have been including Social Thinking® vocabulary and concepts. In defining the script-writing process, I've found it mirrors the values in cooperative and collaborative learning theory. Also incorporated within Social Theatre™ skits and activities are ideas from many social emotional paradigms or programs, such as cognitive behavioral therapy (CBT), Social Thinking®, theory of mind, mindfulness, and assertive-ness training.

CBT, as a cognitive theory of psychology, is ingrained in some of the skits as well as in the script-writing. As CBT focuses on irrational thoughts, cognitive distortions, and defense mechanisms, the brainstorming process can help bring out repressed thoughts as it can be thought of as a group "free association" (Bereiter and Scardamalia 1987). Moreover, the process of allowing and accepting others' ideas, sharing one's own ideas, and the eventual selection of ideas challenges black and white thinking. The realization that not all ideas will fit challenges participants who think they have the best ideas, as Burns (1989) defines in the cognitive distortion of "being right." Other important aspects of cognitive theory utilized in Social Theatre™'s script development process, the improv games, and activities are "cognitive flexibility," as originally described by William Scott (1962), and the idea of "centration," which was derived by Jean Piaget (1972). Scott explains "cognitive flexibility" as how much someone can change their perception when more information is presented to them. "Centration," as explained by Piaget (1972), is a developmental stage when one is not able to see past one focused aspect of a situation. In order to establish more thought flexibility, one must be able to move into being able to see multiple aspects and possibilities in a situation. In Social Theatre™, the collaborative writing process presents opportunities to develop many possibilities in scripts, character perspectives, and the magic trick perspectives of audience and magician. Moreover, the main rule of improvisational theatre games is that all ideas are accepted, which is practice for collaborative idea building and mind flexibility. Participants are also rewarded with acceptance of their own ideas by others, as well as being able to see their final product during a performance. As stated in Centerstage's (n.d.) *Teaching Playwriting in Schools*, participants tend to have difficulty with the editing and revision process, but once participants can see their final product, they appreciate the collaborative efforts that helped get them there.

As the group creates their skits collaboratively, each participant's voice is important. In each process the group members make choices together, and are guided in their thoughts by the group leader. Once the group has established a problem, the group leader can incorporate a specific lesson on the social skill to defeat the defined problem. Together, the group evaluates and utilizes critical thinking skills to choose an ending that can resolve the problem with the use of a social skill. The importance of establishing collaborative learning opportunities is reflected in Gokhale's (1995) research comparing the importance of individual learning and collaborative learning for drill and practice and critical thinking. In detail, Gokhale (1995) found that collaborative learning produced a statistically greater outcome in critical thinking than individual learning.

Gillies (2015) discussed that when learning in a group, structure must be present to define goals and purpose. Furthermore, group participants must be given a task that is doable and attainable, which can help establish participants helping each other (Gillies 2015). With direction and clear expectations about the group goals, Social

Theatre™ participants have been able to work from the brainstorming process all the way to performance of their original skits.

Theory of mind is a concept that was first developed by Premack and Woodruff (1978) in their studies of chimpanzees and behavior. They explained "theory of mind" as the process whereby one's mind recognizes others' feelings and perspectives. Baron-Cohen (1989) found that those with autism spectrum disorder have difficulty with theory of mind, thus exhibiting difficulty with understanding and inferring others' thoughts, feelings, and perspectives. Similarly, Slama *et al.* (2011) found that patients with ADHD also exhibit socio-cognitive difficulties that appear to be connected to theory of mind.

In order to address the theory of mind thought process of understanding others' perspectives, thoughts, and feelings, Social Theatre™ has created and is continuously creating activities to teach and practice social skills. In Social Theatre™, we practice activities with an adjustable pace geared toward group participation, with the purpose of making our own social cues and practicing recognition of the social cues. For example, for those on a lower social-cognitive level, we practice blanket folding or slowly following the hand movements of others to know when we should match the energy of others in helping to fold the blanket. We utilize other activities to practice what feelings look like. More specifically, we practice what awkward looks like, and practice the recognition of others feeling awkward. Then, we incorporate the feelings and reactions of awkwardness into our plays in order to help our participants recognize and understand what this means.

Social learning theorist Albert Bandura (1969) describes three steps that are important in learning through observation, of "vicarious reinforcement," "modeling," and "behavioral rehearsal." Modeling and behavioral rehearsal are essential in Social Theatre™, as being able to practice social skills with others through theatre and script-writing provides a natural outlet. However, for those who struggle more with social-cognitive skills, behavioral rehearsal in itself may not be enough.

MODIFIED IMPROV GAMES FOR DIFFERENT ABILITY LEVELS

In the Social Theatre™ program, I have developed a way to look at improv activities in order to adapt them to a participant's level. In order for participants to learn from improv theatre and other interactive games, it is important to first assess what level participants are at, the skills they have and don't yet have, and adapt improv activities to the basic skill participants need to work on. Once the participants have improved with that skill, another challenge can be added to the improv activity until the participants are ready for the next added challenge to the activity. For example, for participants who do not read social cues very well, they are asked to increase the display of social cues, such as body and facial expression. Later on, the increase in body and facial expression can be decreased. We also have activities where we first use vocal cues to make it more obvious, then decrease to only eye contact. For expressive language delays, the use of activities that will allow participants to act without speaking, then adding gibberish, or one-word answers, and gradually increasing the expectations within the game, can increase verbalizations while maintaining comfort. For participants with anxiety, modifications are done in a similar fashion, instead using graduated exposure techniques (see Chapter Eight).

Learning through experience is essential in Social Theatre™, as groups are continuously moving through Kolb's experiential learning cycle (1984) of "thinking, acting, experiencing, and reflecting" through the script development process, improvisational games, and learning and practicing social skills lessons. Peterson *et al.* (2015) also discuss how merging the theory of movement and learning is helpful to explain kinesthetic learning styles. Even in the roots of the Social Theatre™ program, we have learned about the program and idea development through thinking, acting, experiencing, and reflecting. Through the movement of doing and experiencing, we continue to learn and experience collaborative social skills development together.

"MY IDEA" VERSUS "OUR IDEAS" AS BUILDING BLOCKS

In the helping and teaching professions, we know many of our children and teens struggle socially due to difficulties caused by their lack of collaboration skills. Many of our students will become stuck on their own ideas, not being able to let go or accept others' ideas. However, Aristotle's reference to the entirety of a product, and not a focus on individualism, said it best: "the totality is not, as it were, a mere heap, but the whole is something besides the parts" (from Aristotle 1981 (trans.)).

In Social Theatre™, we see ideas as puzzle pieces that may or may not fit together, which eventually become a product. Furthermore, all ideas are accepted and are important.

Buchs and Butera (in Gillies 2015, p.213) found that students struggle with cooperative learning in the classroom even with cooperative skills training, due to "social comparison." On the other hand, Plato discusses in *The Republic* (1989 (trans.), 349d–e) that a musician and a physician hold equal importance and knowledge, and one is not more important than the other. Instead of encouraging an environment where participants feel competition or social comparison, Social Theatre™'s philosophy is active and collaborative participation, thus we accept all ideas as equal and important.

In Social Theatre™, participants learn to let go of their "my idea" type of thinking and adapt to the group and "our ideas." The participants learn to accept others' ideas more, and the ultimate goal is for participants to understand that everyone's ideas are building blocks to a finished product.

SETTING THE PURPOSE AND MOTIVATION

Using visual, auditory, and kinesthetic learning styles, Social Theatre™ can be a way for those who struggle with social deficits to learn and practice social skills. Writing sketch comedy about our own social mistakes can be a way to practice better social skills and learn how to have humor about everyday social faux pas.

Moreover, this environment is created by sharing the purpose of the group with the participants. The purpose of the group is to congruently help participants to learn and practice their own social skills while writing and performing plays that teach others about the social skills participants have learned about. As role models, they will teach social skills to others, while practicing these skills themselves, in preparation for teaching others. In the closing session of the group, a short performance may be given for a chosen audience. In schools, the audience can be chosen grades, the entire school, or the local community. For private practice (with proper parental consent), nursing homes or special recreation programs are a wonderful outlet, in which the participants can practice conversational skills through conversation and even demonstrate magic tricks with audience members after performances.

Chapter Two

THE CREATION
OF GROUPS

Since I have been running my afterschool Social Theatre™ program I have been witness to many obstacles and many successes based upon the makeup of my groups. In my mixed social level afterschool program, I have witnessed students help each other and become accepting of each other regardless of differences in social level. On the other hand, concepts and even theatre games taught in mixed groups might be not challenging enough for some, while too difficult for others to understand. In private practice, I have grouping Social Theatre™ participants by social-cognitive level. Increasingly, many programs are grouping by social-cognitive level (Baker 2003; Chasen 2011; Winner 2013). Chasen (2011) also follows a similar model in which the drama therapy grouping is geared toward children with high functioning spectrum disorders. In Social Theatre™, many of the strategies in this book can be utilized across the spectrum. For ease of use, strategies and plays from Social Theatre™ are categorized according to social-cognitive level (see Breakdown Chart by Social Thinking® Profile Level and Target Skills). Grouping the participants according to their social level has had a dramatic effect on how much we have been able to accomplish within Social Theatre™ groups.

Social Theatre™ is valuable to all levels, but throughout the chapters, activities are broken down to accommodate those on different social-cognitive levels. There are activities that have been modified for participants on a lower social-cognitive level to learn and practice theory of mind skills, including joint focus, eye contact, feelings recognition, and recognizing social cues. When participants have a higher social-cognitive level, the activities can be modified with greater challenges to increase skills in the areas of feelings recognition, eye contact, joint focus, recognizing social cues, perspective taking, and collaborative imagination. The chart shows how the activities are grouped according to the levels of the social mind, outlined in the Social Thinking® Social Communication Profile at Socialthinking.com (Winner, Crooke, and Madrigal n.d.). The following discussion addresses group size, but as a rule of thumb, for those with more challenges, smaller groups are always better.

SOCIAL THINKING® SOCIAL COMMUNICATION PROFILE: HELPFUL IN DEVELOPING SOCIAL THEATRE™ THERAPY GROUPS

If the environment and the makeup of the pool of participants allows it, the creation of groups divided according to social-cognitive level helps immensely. Professionals are increasingly grouping by social-cognitive levels, and many have found it helpful in order to create lessons geared toward participants. In the book *Why Teach Social Thinking®?* (2013), Michelle Garcia Winner explains that labels do not give enough information in order to be able to establish social-cognitive leveled groups. Winner, Crooke, and Madrigal (n.d.) created the Social Thinking® Social Communication Profile to present a structured explanation of the social difficulties individuals face, as expressed through their six levels of the social mind:

1. Significantly Challenged Social Communicator

2. Challenged Social Communicator

3. Emerging Social Communicator

4. Nuance Challenged Social Communicator

     i.   Weak Interactive Social Communicator

     ii. Socially Anxious Social Communicator

5. Neurotypical Social Communicator

6. Resistant Social Communicator.

For Social Theatre™, three of these categories are described, as these are most applicable to those grouped in therapeutic settings, and these are utilized in defining and leveling improv techniques in this book (see Breakdown Chart by Social Thinking® Profile Level and Target Skills). The other categories Winner and colleagues address are "Significantly Challenged Social Communicators," "Neurotypical Social Communicators," and "Resistant Social Communicators." Those who are Significantly Challenged Social Communicators have difficulty in a group due to challenges with sensory impairments, severe language impairments or non-verbal language, and self-regulation, thus work best individually. Neurotypical Social Communicators are those who have appropriate social skills and communication for their age range. These are the participants of Social Theatre™ who have typically been in the afterschool program, which is not a therapeutic setting, and have taken leadership roles in creating and performing plays. All of the activities in this book and in the program can be utilized with Neurotypical Social Communicators. For those who would fall into the Resistant Social Communicator category, the Social Theatre™ group would not be able to effectively attend to their needs and would not be helpful for them. Resistant Social Communicators are those who tend to want to be in control of the group and, if challenged in a group context, act as if, or verbalize that, they do not care how others feel.

Most importantly, I have found that grouping participants by social-cognitive level has allowed us to focus on skills in a deeper level at a pace the participants can understand. When I have mixed groups, such as in my afterschool program where there are varied levels, it is difficult to ensure that all of the participants understand the concepts. Therefore, when possible, utilizing social-cognitive leveled groups is recommended. To obtain more information on the Social Thinking® Social Communication Profile—levels of the social mind, read the comprehensive article of the same name at Socialthinking.com. For a helpful assessment tool, see the book *Thinking About You, Thinking About Me* (Winner, 2007), in particular, the "Social Dynamic Assessment Protocol."

Challenged Social Communicators (Social Thinking® Social Communication Profile)

Winner, Crooke, and Madrigal (n.d.) describe the characteristics of those who fall into this category as individuals who experience anxiety over environment changes, can be overwhelmed in less structured social situations, can be sensory seeking when overwhelmed, perseverate on self-interests, have difficulty attending in a classroom, are weak in joint focus abilities, and struggle with theory of mind. Some in this category struggle with separating fact and fiction, and have a history of expressive/receptive language challenges. From a young age, this group of individuals has been recognized as having autism. "Challenged Social Communicators" can be taught the basic concept of others having a perspective as a way to help the person, without necessarily expecting mastery of the skill.

Challenged Social Communicators are typically good at concrete types of thinking, and may therefore present stronger skills in reading, decoding, and math computation. However, reading comprehension can be a weak area because of difficulty understanding inferences.

Grouping those who are Challenged Social Communicators (Social Thinking® Social Communication Profile)

When working with Challenged Social Communicators, it is important to work in small groups of two or three so as to be able to focus on skills for each participant. In group, begin with simple games (found later in the book) such as Scarf Juggling, Blanket Folding, Playing Boo, Mirroring, Voice Levels, simple Feelings Charades (happy, sad, mad), or the Slow Motion Snowball Fight. These games help participants practice eye contact, joint focus, recognizing feelings and social cues, and reacting to another's play. Moreover, these are also activities that can help work on understanding one's body and voice within a mutual space. When ready for more of a challenge, these participants can try Room Chi, and The Martha Game (found later in the book), Dance Party, and Using Stage Levels. For Challenged Social Communicators, their struggles with theory of mind and perseveration of ideas make collaborative writing and brainstorming very difficult. Moreover, having this group of participants participate in acting out ineffective behaviors could backfire, as they might grasp on to the humor without understanding why ineffective behavior is demonstrated. Therefore, the second half of skits that teach correct behaviors can be taught to this group.

In order to be inclusive, a leader can invite the group categorized as Challenged Social Communicators to the performance. They are able to participate in the larger group performing the Slow Motion Snowball Fight and in the resolution of Call Me When You're Down paired with the other participants when inviting the sad actor/actress to hang out. Moreover, the Dance Party activity can be a fun on-stage activity for participants of all levels to conclude the performance with.

Emerging Social Communicators (Social Thinking® Social Communication Profile)

Individuals in the "Emerging Social Communicators" profile (Winner, Crooke, and Madrigal n.d.; Socialthinking.com) tend to appear awkward and struggle to follow the line of communication. Oftentimes, individuals in this category have the tendency to make off-topic comments and their voice patterns may be irregular in terms of pitch, rhythm, or volume. As individuals in this group mature, they may be able to make their sensory difficulties more subtle, but may still have a stiff posture and/or movements. In larger group settings, such as classrooms, attention and focus can be difficult especially during group projects or less structured discussions. During classroom lectures, these individuals can attend but may need cueing if they interrupt or talk too long. Literal language interpretation is a trend due to difficulty with inferencing, but this can also improve. Individuals in this group tend to have more social interest than Challenged Social Communicators and with therapy this group can learn more interaction skills and more understanding of theory of mind. However, the processing of social information most likely takes longer for those in this group in comparison to those in the "Weak Interactive Social Communicators" profile.

Gifts that Emerging Social Communicators may possess are high intelligence, humor, and attention to detail. These communicators also tend to have a concrete type of thinking, and therefore may present stronger skills in reading, decoding, and math computation.

Grouping those who are Emerging Social Communicators (Social Thinking® Social Communication Profile)

When working with older Emerging Social Communicators (junior high and above) all of the activities can be utilized. An ideal group within this category would include three or four participants. Older participants from this group can typically understand humor and can be taught that some of our skits demonstrate blatantly ineffective social skills, and typically understand that these ineffective skills are not to be repeated off stage. In fact, acting out reactions to ineffective and awkward social skills can really help individuals within this group to recognize others' reactions and possible perceptions.

With this group, preparation for brainstorming and collaborative creation must be an emphasis for three or more sessions before attempting brainstorming. This would include teaching about the rules for brainstorming and deleted scenes (see Chapter Three) to demonstrate that every idea is valued but sometimes an idea does not fit. The idea book would also be discussed and students can start to use it when they have an idea for brainstorming—even when the group is doing an activity, the student can write down their idea instead of going off-topic.

Once these steps have been taken, brainstorming can start. The first few times the group brainstorms, the sessions may be short, increasing in duration over the next few sessions. One important trend that may continuously resurface in working with this group is the need for help to understand the difference between on-task and off-task statements. This is also important during script development, and Emerging Social Communicators will need more guidance and ideas in helping them group ideas that match, and eventually the provision of more cues to help their ideas flow into a play. Moreover, this group may also need more time discussing flexibility and how all ideas are great, but some do not fit in the current play being created.

Nuance Challenged Social Communicators (Social Thinking® Social Communication Profile)

"Nuance Challenged Social Communicators" are defined by Winner, Crooke, and Madrigal (n.d.; Socialthinking.com) as those who exhibit slightly awkward social skills, and the slight awkwardness can go unnoticed. Two types of "challenged communicators" are defined underneath this category: those who are weak in communication skills and those who are anxious socially.

Grouping those who are Nuance Challenged Social Communicators (Social Thinking® Social Communication Profile)

All of the activities in this book are appropriate for Nuance Challenged Social Communicators. This group will also do very well in the collaborative writing process from brainstorming through performance.

SMALL GROUP FORMAT (FOR THERAPY GROUPS)

When meeting with a small group, the following format of activities can help to keep participants active and focused. A typical session is 45–50 minutes total, with an optional parent wrap up at the end. The group can begin with informal conversation, where everyone takes time to share details about their week, and others are encouraged to ask questions or share validating comments. Next, a social emotional concept chosen by the professional is taught with group discussion following. If a good idea comes up during discussion, write it on the whiteboard, or have the participant write it on a Post-it® to keep for the brainstorming session. The improvisational theatre game can give participants an opportunity to think about or practice the skill learned in the lesson, or at the very least, provide a brain break. Then, brainstorming and script-writing (see Chapter Three) can begin or continue from the last week. Any ideas that were given during the lesson discussion can be added onto a previous brainstorming list, or written on the top of the list. When participants seem out of ideas or as if they are losing interest, tell them to think about more ideas or details over the week. Then, move on to learning a skit or practicing a skit that has been written or is in the process of being evaluated (see Chapter Three, Fifth Step). After all of the activity, I find some of my participants are at an elevated level of excitement, therefore doing a mindfulness activity together is helpful. When parents are involved, they are also very grateful to have calmer participants afterwards, as well as being appreciative of any new strategies to incorporate at home.

The structure of the session

- Informal conversation (includes cues, praise, and encouragements to utilize skills).

- Teach and practice social emotional concept with visuals.

- Improvisational theatre game (replace with teaching new skits when more time is needed).

- Brainstorming/collaborative script-writing.

- Learn skit or practice new skit.

- End with 1–2-minute mindfulness skill.

Optional: wrap up with parents to discuss skills practiced in session. Give assignment for the week.

Larger group format for an afterschool program

In an afterschool program with Neurotypical and Nuance Challenged Social Communicators (as conceptualized by Winner, Crooke, and Madrigal n.d.), it is possible to work with up to 10–12 students. Even when one or two Emerging Social Communicators (Winner, Crooke, and Madrigal n.d.) want to join, I would include them. However, including participants with more needs could require more leaders. An alternative is to recruit mature and neurotypical participants who can take on a leadership role in helping those with more needs.

If in a mixed Social Theatre™ group, Emerging Social Communicators will need further work in a small group to understand some of the basic concepts the afterschool program is working on, otherwise they might feel anxious and overwhelmed at not understanding at the speed of the others.

In a larger group of more than ten participants, brainstorming and collaborative script-writing can be difficult. If there are varied attendance days, brainstorming, grouping of ideas, and evaluating ideas would be more effective when there are fewer than eight participants. If there are not varied attendance days, brainstorming, grouping of ideas, and evaluating ideas can be done in a smaller group. Once ideas have been more formulated in the smaller group, they can be taken to the larger afterschool group to ask what they like and what they would improve.

Teaching and utilizing the collaborative writing process in small groups throughout the school or engaging a classroom in the collaborative writing process can be mutually beneficial as skits can be produced and introduced during the afterschool process. I always include everyone in the afterschool program, but I sometimes utilize my time with small groups to teach collaboration through writing the basis of skits. We then take these skit ideas to the larger afterschool program and allow students the choice of adding characterizations and lines that match the situations.

CLASSROOM GROUP FORMAT

Whether it is a smaller or larger classroom, students can be grouped into three or four and taught the brainstorming and collaborative script-writing process. With Nuance Challenged and Neurotypical student groups, students may be able to function with minimal guidance through the process. With those who have greater social challenges, they will need more support and possibly even to work in a dyad with or without adult support, or individually with an adult to guide the process.

In a smaller classroom, the teaching staff can lead the process of brainstorming through script development, whereas in a larger classroom the teaching staff can oversee the students working together. If this is too advanced a skill for students to work together more independently, again, the process can be taught in a smaller setting.

Chapter Three

THE COLLABORATIVE SCRIPT-WRITING PROCESS

One of the essential parts of Social Theatre™ is the collaborative script-writing process, which was discovered through our "unofficial" ethnographic study of the program, conducted with the students with parent permission in 2008. This initial discovery was made by analyzing and grouping brainstorming session writings, individual writings/ideas, and scripts. The process of brainstorming through to script-writing has been honed over the years alongside participants, and the following is what we have been using effectively for the past few years.

Through the collaborative script-writing process, participants are led through the process of creating a play together. Script-writing allows participants to utilize their creativity as well as applying social skills lessons they have learned. However, with any collaborative process there is an expectation of flexibility and willingness to give and take.

IMPORTANT TRENDS TO REMEMBER

1. Skits need to be clear and simple for the audience to understand.

2. Skits must also be simple and short.

3. Skits should include a blank canvas to allow character development, but maintain a basic storyline.

4. Solidified and written skits can always be made better with more character development, more humor, more social concept clarity, but will always follow the same storyline.

There are many challenges to this process. Participants sometimes think their ideas are the best. Sometimes it is difficult for participants to move past their own ideas and accept others' ideas. Listening to criticism to help script flow, allowing ideas to be merged, and accepting characters developing differently from the way they had envisioned can be difficult for group members. However, it has been my experience, and has been discussed in *Teaching Playwriting in Schools: Teacher's Handbook* (Centerstage n.d.), that through the process, participants can learn the value of being able to work through challenges to produce an amazing result. This chapter will give ideas on how to help participants through the process of developing plays under Social Theatre™'s specific model of collaborative playwriting.

FIRST STEP: BRAINSTORMING RULES

In order to get the most out of the brainstorming process, rules for brainstorming must be discussed.

The most important rule in the brainstorming process is to maintain an environment where everyone's ideas are valued. Participants need to feel comfortable to take risks in sharing their ideas. Linker's (2010) article is utilized to provide the basis of our brainstorming rules, but simplified for those who might also struggle with attending and/or remembering.

1. No judging ideas.

2. No discussing or evaluating ideas until later.

3. Don't discuss too many details until later.

4. No commenting except for positive comments such as "Cool, wow, great idea! Ooohh…"

If any of these rules are violated, Linker (2010) explains that the idea flow is obstructed. This is evident, and oftentimes I have to redirect my groups to stay with the brainstorming process as they get very excited about specific ideas and want to build right away on one specific idea, although this might not be the path the story takes. Initially spending too much time on one idea can end up being a time waster. Moreover, teaching the participants to begin by brainstorming main ideas can also teach self-control.

Individuals with spectrum disorders and social difficulties can have challenges with understanding perspective and sometimes perseverance on their own ideas, which also refers to how flexibly someone thinks. When there is limited cognitive flexibility, the participant presents with more obstacles and would need to focus only on improvisation skills and practicing skits in order to learn about sharing ideas and collaborating in a group. When the participants can be more flexible and accepting of others' ideas, the brainstorming process toward script-writing can start. At times, just the process of brainstorming itself can create collaboration, even if it means a script does not necessarily come out of the brainstorming. In a day camp, I taught improv to a group of young adults who would have been categorized under the Social Thinking® Social Communication Profile as Challenged Social Communicators. The setting included a similar aged helper with every group of three or four adults. I challenged the group to brainstorm their favorite ideas and put them into a skit. Since this group tended to perseverate on their own ideas, their skits did not make sense; however, the leaders helped their groups put their ideas together and they performed their skits anyway. One of the skits was about a couch (someone acted like a couch), another person was a dog (sitting on the couch), and there was an airplane (buzzing around the area). After the participants performed their skits, they were incredibly proud of themselves and each other. In short, even though some participants have more challenges, there is remarkable value in having these participants be part of a short brainstorming process and performing their ideas together during group sessions.

When writing plays together, we utilize each other's ideas as building blocks in brainstorming, creating, and acting. Cohen (2011, p.133) discusses that the safety actors feel is what enables collaboration, but this can be torn down altogether if actors compete for attention instead of working with each other. At times children may even become frustrated when they realize others like and use their ideas. In collaborative script-writing, there is no such thing as copying. This can also be explained as part of the rules for the writing process.

Expect interrupting and overlapping

Understanding the process of brainstorming can also be somewhat difficult for those with social deficits, as there is natural excitement that leads to overlapping and interrupting. Vass *et al.* (2008) discusses that interrupting and overlapping is typical during brainstorming. Therefore, prepare participants for overlapping and interrupting to be viewed as normal during brainstorming, rather than being viewed as disrespectful.

Brainstorming like free association

Bereiter and Scardamalia (1987) discussed that brainstorming is much like free association. In my groups, I have found my students and participants have discussed deeper issues. The following are all real examples of topics that have come out of our brainstorming sessions: bullying, teasing, differences, making problems worse, grieving, policing others' behavior, being bossy, bragging, spatial issues, rambling in conversation, perseveration on one topic, and feelings. After getting an initial list of topics, group members are asked to give examples of all of the ideas that have been listed. They are not told to share personal examples, but more often than not they do share personal examples. In one example, a group member discussed a traumatic time when he was chased. Others have discussed in more detail their experiences of being bullied, being left out, and fear of having socially awkward moments.

SECOND STEP: TWO QUESTIONS TO BRAINSTORM

First question

What are the topics kids your age need to learn about?

I have found that participants will discuss any of their issues when asked this question, as they think they are talking about topics "other kids" need to learn about. The idea of collaborating about one's own issues in the third person is supported in Hsing's (2015) study about self-perception and affect. University students were asked to recall embarrassing moments by writing in the first person versus the third person. In third-person writings, the participants wrote about themselves in a more positive light, having coped with the experiences in a more positive light.

Second question

What are awkward, embarrassing moments, or social mistakes?

I have been asked how we can make the brainstorming of certain topics humorous, such as someone being alone at lunch. In order to do this, we must identify what the missing skill is that has created the awkward or embarrassing moment.

When we identify what the missing skill is, we can exaggerate the awkward behavior and write a skit about the skill. One format of a play is to include the effective and ineffective ways people try to perform a social task. See the plays "Wanna Hang Out?" (Chapter Five) and "7 Ways to Defeat a Bully" (Chapter Nine) for examples.

Idea book

Keep a book of ideas from the brainstorming process. Every idea is to be written on a Post-it® and organized into one of two categories in the book. Identical to the two brainstorming questions, the two categories are:

1. Topics people need to learn about.

2. Awkward, embarrassing moments, or social mistakes.

By this time, the participants most likely understand that all ideas are great; it's just that some do not fit the puzzle. If their idea is not utilized for the play the group is working on presently, it will stay in the book to be utilized later in the current group, or maybe in a future group with the same or different participants.

THIRD STEP: PREPARATION FOR EVALUATING, INCREASING COGNITIVE FLEXIBILITY

The concept of cognitive flexibility was originally coined by William Scott (1962) through research about sorting, which led to the understanding of a range of difficulties for different people. Moreover, the concept of cognitive flexibility further explained with what level of ease or difficulty one can expand or flex one's mind to adapt to new or different information.

The evaluation of ideas step can challenge participants' flexibility. Before evaluating, choosing, or bringing ideas together, participants must be prepared and ready to be flexible.

In order to prepare participants for this process:

- Discuss that *all* ideas are valuable! Even movie creators have ideas they can't use. Ideas are like random puzzle pieces— some ideas fit, some do not.

- Show deleted scenes from movies, which can be found by searching on the internet, typing in the name of a movie with the phrase "deleted scenes" afterward. My personal favorite deleted scene examples are songs that didn't make it into the movie *Frozen*, which are on the second CD on the *Frozen* soundtrack (2013), and the *Inside Out Deleted Scenes: Cast's Favourite* (2015), which can be found on YouTube.

FOURTH STEP: GROUP IDEAS FROM BRAINSTORMS
Keep an ongoing online document

As we start grouping, we look at our brainstorms in the idea book. I have the participants take the Post-it® notes and put them into categories on the wall. We type the groups of ideas into an online document, which can become the beginning puzzle pieces of skits. This document can also be shared with group members—not to edit, but to add comments and other ideas that can possibly be included later.

When teaching the skill, the group leader can incorporate knowledge of their own to teach social emotional concepts within their group's plays. In the plays that follow this chapter, we have utilized concepts from Social Thinking®, theory of mind, CBT, mindfulness, and other sources, which can be utilized to teach and explain how to perform the skill effectively. These concepts are explained before each play, and discussion questions you can ask your group to help with and assess their understanding of the concepts are provided.

After grouping ideas, it might become clearer to the leader which ideas the group is moving toward. The group will most likely have more excitement about one of the ideas, or grouped ideas. They are then ready to move on to the next step.

FIFTH STEP: VALIDATING EACH OTHER'S IDEAS WHILE EVALUATING, AND RE-WRITING

In this phase, participants will look at the list of groups they came up with in the previous step. Participants volunteer to try out chosen ideas on stage. Seeing participants' ideas in action helps to solidify the ideas that fit into the puzzle and those that do not. In order to gain more ideas, the participants watching those on stage are asked to discuss what they liked about what those on stage did. Then, when compliments are given, thought bubbles are utilized to ask what others might be thinking about those who just gave compliments.

When all of the participants on stage have received a compliment, others are asked to evaluate by sharing their opinions. They are asked to discuss what an audience's perspective might be, and what they might do to make the skit more understandable and even better.

This third step of validating, practicing, and evaluating is repeated for each segment of a skit until the skit is complete.

The following are ways that Social Theatre™ plays are formatted. There is always a narrator, who plays the very important role of teaching the social emotional concepts. During the last part of a play demonstrating correct behavior, participants who are Challenged Social Communicators can participate.

Two Social Theatre™ typical skit formats

1. Wrong behavior >> narrator freeze and discuss >> right behavior.

2. Show many ineffective social skills >> narrator freeze each time >> last time effective social skill *(Examples: "7 Ways to Defeat a Bully" and "Wanna Hang Out?").*

Copying and story creation

Oftentimes, when participants discuss or present an idea, others will also like the idea. When others like an idea, they will sometimes use the idea as part of a play. All ideas belong to everyone in the group. Therefore, when an idea is shared in a collaborative process, the idea can be utilized however the idea fits within the play. Another way to view someone else using someone's idea is as a collaborative process of presenting the idea through to completion with someone executing the idea on stage. Even though the participant with the original idea may not be actually performing the idea, the person behind the creation of the story is just as important as the performer.

SIXTH STEP: ROLE ASSIGNMENT

In order to encourage perspective taking in all of the different roles, parts are not assigned until two weeks before performance. This also makes it easier when the group needs to be flexible, as if participants are not able to attend performances at the last minute, others can easily be assigned to other parts to cover for who is missing.

Scripts are written when the skit is solidified after going through the process of evaluation, practice, and re-evaluation. A chosen and neutral participant can then write the skit or the skit can be written by the leader. The skit can then be practiced with the script a couple of times, and then the script is to be taken away to increase improvisational skills. In each skit, participants are encouraged to remember the events that occur, not to memorize their lines. If they can remember what occurs, they can interject the appropriate comments and actions in order to demonstrate the scenes.

Many participants have told me they are not good at memorizing lines. However, participants are more confident once they understand they just need to memorize the situation and not the lines. When memorizing the situation, participants verbalize accordingly and can help each other through the scene. If a group needs it, I will write the cues backstage to help them remember, and during practice the cues will be available until not needed.

Here's a memory trick for a no script example

The breakdown of "Big Problem or Little Problem?" (in Chapter Six) is this:

1. Grand Canyon fall—BIG PROBLEM, small reaction.

2. Grand Canyon fall—BIG PROBLEM, BIG REACTION.

3. Pencil breaks—small problem, BIG REACTION.

4. Pencil breaks—small problem, small reaction.

Chapter Four

ACTIVITIES/SKITS TO TEACH JOINT ATTENTION AND FOCUS

When acting on stage or being part of an improvisational game, participants must utilize joint attention and focus. Theory of mind (Premack and Woodruff 1978) establishes the concept that cognitive functions are used to recognize others' perceptions through environmental information and feelings recognition. Similarly, Mundy (2016) points out that joint attention is deeper than only reciprocal or structured attention, as it is necessary to pay attention to many different factors in the environment at once, which may be hard for those who have difficulty with processing information.

When everyone is attending, improvisation can gain momentum and participants will have even more fun together. Since most of Social Theatre™'s work is with participants who have social difficulties, more involved improvisational games can be overwhelming. Therefore, what I am including are games we created, basic improvisational games, and adapted improvisational games.

THE MARTHA GAME

Even though the origin is unknown, The Martha Game is a staple to improv and is well known (Buchanan n.d.). The Martha Game is a wonderful tool for practicing joint attention, quick thinking, using body expression, sharing an imagination, and being on topic.

A theme (e.g. zoo) is chosen by the leader or by the first participant. The first participant goes up to the front and says "I'm a lion" and poses as a lion to match the theme, and freezes. The next participant walks up to the front and says "I'm a fence" and poses as a fence. The third participant walks up to the front and says "I'm a zookeeper "and poses as a zookeeper. The game goes on until the last participant poses. The goal is to have the game happen rather quickly without pauses.

The group can also be challenged by asking their characters to interact with each other once the last person has posed.

PLAYING BOO

In order to create simple and reciprocal play, this activity can be used with those who have a more challenged cognitive disability or for younger participants aged 2 and up.

In order to increase playfulness and excitement over the activity, have participants wear some accessories such as a hat, a clown nose, and clown glasses. If full clown costumes are available, this can create even more excitement.

Model the behavior before having the participants try. Hold a curtain in between two participants. Remove the curtain, and one participant yells "Boo!" The other participant has to act surprised and create a reaction. Praise participants afterwards and ask if it was fun to play with their friends. Tell them when they play together it makes them happy.

MIRRORING

Mirroring is a basic and well known theatre activity (Gesell 1997) in which participants are placed into pairs. Each team chooses someone to be the one who is gazing in the mirror, and the other is the mirror. The "mirror" must follow every movement and facial expression.

An adaptation of this game, which is for those who need more challenge, is to try to start "speaking in one voice."

Next challenge: Two people who were mirroring each other practice speaking in one voice.

Next challenge: Three people mirror each other.

Next challenge: Three people mirror each other and speak in one voice.

Next challenge: Speed up the voice!

Next challenge: Three people mirror each other and speak in one voice while trying to tell a story.

Next challenge: Have one pair or trio who can mirror each other and speak together in the same voice communicate with another pair or trio.

FOUNDATION IMPROV ACTIVITY

Because many who struggle with social deficits have difficulty knowing when to talk, they sometimes interrupt or are overly cautious when verbally entering a conversation. In teaching improv, I find that sometimes we even need to back up to practice the foundation improv activity, as participants will regress and forget how they need to share the stage with their bodies and with their vocalizations.

In teaching visual cues during improv, I have the participants go through the initial steps of:

- recognizing when someone wants to speak

- recognizing whose turn it is next

- recognizing the meaning of others' body expression.

We practice what someone looks like when they want to speak, giving everyone a chance to show how they look and how others look when they want to speak.

In improvisational activities, one must notice when a person has stepped forward, which means it is their turn to talk and act. We practice this basic skill in many of the improvisation games, and if it is a more difficult skill for some, we practice it by itself first. Once the group becomes acclimated to stepping forward and noticing others stepping forward, increase the challenge by not having others step forward so participants notice only body language and voice as indicators of whose turn it is next.

BACKGROUND OF SLOW MOTION SNOWBALL FIGHT

The Slow Motion Snowball Fight was created by the Sahs Clown (now Comedy Improv) Troupe in 2006 as part of "7 Ways to Defeat a Bully" (Chapter Nine). However, over the years, it has become a tool in itself to teach joint attention, reciprocal play, non-verbal communication, and collaboration.

It's always important to teach the basic skill through a small role-play first. Ask a participant to improvise with the leader. Have the student react to the leader's snowballs, while the leader is not reacting to any snowballs and is just throwing snowballs. Then, ask those watching who is more fun to play with: someone who reacts to the snowballs or someone who doesn't react.

SLOW MOTION SNOWBALL FIGHT

Objective: To increase joint attention; at a deeper level, to read non-verbal cues of others in order to react; and, at an even deeper level, to read cues of others in order to non-verbally and cooperatively plan an ending.

In the background: "Chariots of Fire" song (Vangelis 1981).

Students utilize all of their stage presence levels, utilizing slow motion and capturing every small, exaggerated movement. Each student chooses another student with eye contact, which the other student reciprocates. The student picks up snow, packs it, and with mutual eye contact, throws the snowball at the other student. The other student chooses how to react—to duck, or to let it hit them. Students are encouraged to use facial expression, or even slow motion words. If there is room, they can even fall in slow motion. They also need to pay attention to where others are placed on the stage in order to ensure that everyone can be seen by the audience.

Students can pick another student to throw a snowball at, or reciprocate. Toward the end of the song, students can non-verbally decide how to cooperatively end the snowball fight—with a truce, with other students downed and one victor, cheering together, walking off together, walking away in teams, walking away separately, etc.

Differentiated learning

Level 1: Pair students up, make eye contact, and throw snowballs in slow motion with reactions to snowballs.

Level 2: In bigger groups, partner students to utilize mutual eye contact and react to snowballs in slow motion.

Level 3: You can use even larger groups, but challenge them by allowing group members to alternate whom they are throwing snowballs at. Individuals must watch the eye gaze and actions of others to decide whose snowballs to react to.

Level 4: The group chooses an ending with some verbal cues and planning beforehand.

Level 5: The group chooses an ending with non-verbal cues and no planning beforehand.

DANCE PARTY

Techno or other fun, danceable music playing.

Each person takes a turn to teach a goofy dance move; the group follows the dance move, then passes leadership on to the next person with an arm movement presenting the next person.

Next challenge: Pass leadership with only eye contact.

MINDFULNESS WITH OTHERS: SCARF JUGGLING—1-2-3 THROW

Level 1 explores Michelle Garcia Winner's vocabulary concept of "thinking with your eyes" (Winner 2007) and at Levels 2 and 3 her concept of being a "Just me" vs. a "Thinking about you" person is incorporated into the teaching. Winner explains that a "Just me" person acts in their own interests, not recognizing others' interests. Furthermore, when a person becomes a "Thinking about you" person, they are increasingly recognizing others' interests, feelings, and perspectives. In order to help a participant learn this concept, they must first utilize joint attending skills, which can help the participant look at others' eye gaze direction and facial expression to decipher feelings.

Differentiated Learning
Level 1
"Just me" concept. At this level, participants are self-directing their own scarf play. Then, teach the class as a whole "1-2-3 Throw!" Encourage the students to say "1-2-3 Throw" and throw their scarf according to their own timing.

To process: How did you feel throwing the scarf? Was it fun to be by yourself? Would it be more fun to be with someone or by yourself? How would you like to try throwing your scarves with a partner?

Level 2
Beginning of "Thinking about you" skill 1-2-3 Throw (mutual eye contact, the students say "1-2-3 Throw" together, and throw their scarves together).

To process: How did you feel throwing your scarf with your partner? How did your partner feel throwing the scarf with you? How was your partner feeling? How do you know what your partner was feeling? Were you able to throw the scarves at exactly the same time? What tools did you need to figure out when the scarf was going to be thrown? Did you find it easy or difficult? Who thought it was more fun to throw scarves with a partner? Why?

Level 3
Intermediate "Thinking about you" skill. Partners throw their separate scarves together at the same time by only watching each other's body language, facial expression, and using eye contact.

To process: How did you feel trying to communicate without using words? How did your partner feel? How do you know? What did you find challenging? What did you find easier? Do you feel it was more fun or less fun communicating with your body language and facial expressions? Why? Why is this important?

Level 4
Advanced "Thinking about you" and "Thinking with your eyes." Increase the group sizes by one person until the entire group is back together. For less of a challenge, you can revert back to stating together "1-2-3 Throw," or for more of a challenge, have the entire group communicate non-verbally throwing the scarves together at the same time.

To process: How did you feel about throwing the scarves together as a big group? How did you feel as the group became larger? What do you think others felt as the group became larger? What did you notice others doing that helped you? What did you do in an effort to help others understand you? What is the importance of this activity?

BLANKET FOLDING

Izzy Gesell (1997) identifies the game of "blanket folding" as a way to increase teamwork and group completion of goals. This improvisational theatre game focuses on a group folding an imaginary blanket. However, for many folding an imaginary blanket would be difficult due to this game's focus on recognizing social cues, maintaining attention, and keeping the same momentum and energy as the other group members.

As an adaptation, I have begun using a real blanket of which each participant gets two corners. If more of a challenge is needed, each participant gets one corner. We work slowly, recognizing the movements of others, which helps us to know which way to move our hands and bodies. When the group members are folding the blanket, the leader can step in to demonstrate what "unmatched" energy feels like to others. When the leader goes too slow, doesn't move at all, or goes too fast, the group members will moan or laugh. At this point, ask questions:

- What happened?

- What was I doing?

- What did you feel when I was not matching everyone else's speed and energy?

- Are there times when others have not matched your energy or vice versa?

- How did that make you feel?

- I noticed some of you laughed. Does that mean you thought it was funny or were you uncomfortable?

Okay! Let's try it again, matching everyone's energy!

Once smooth, we can get faster and faster. The ultimate goal is to be able to mime folding a blanket with each other, but for some, folding a physical blanket smoothly in a group of three or four is something to be very proud of in itself.

SELF-MONITORING AND ADJUSTING BEHAVIOR THROUGH "ROOM CHI"

In Chinese philosophy, it is important to find the life source within oneself, and one's body. The recognition of feelings within the body is important and having strong chi leads to better health and focus (Energy Arts n.d.). In borrowing this concept, I am relating the "life force" and energy flow to a social situation. When socializing, one must recognize the energy flow in the group or in a room in order to assess what to do next. Theory of mind (Premack and Woodruff 1978) is a concept that encompasses the ability to recognize that others have feelings, needs, and beliefs, as well as being able to connect the information with cues in the environment. The Social Formula from *You Are a Social Detective* (Winner and Crooke 2008) is created as a visual to show how to use your eyes, ears, and brain to configure a social situation. In this exercise, participants can blindly step into a situation where they will have to "use their tools" to understand what they have to do.

Have one student step out of the room while others in the room set up an action, feeling, or both. An example would be showing excitement by talking loudly about their favorite topic. The other person can then join the group, and try to show the same kind of energy. In a reverse example, the group might show sadness, talking about someone's dog running away. The person who rejoins the group needs to be able to recognize the level of the noise in the room, the emotions, and the actions of the others in order to join the group by correctly mirroring these feelings and behaviors.

"THE BUZZ KILL"

"The Buzz Kill" is also known as killing the moment: when someone says or does something that brings down the positive energy in the environment. Depending on the situation, people who kill the moment can also be referred to as Debbie Downer, Negative Nelly, or Gloomy Gus.

Walking into a social situation and being able to focus on and decipher the energy and flow of each social situation is important. In the following skits, "The Buzz Kill" is addressed and how it can ruin a social situation and make others feel uncomfortable.

GO WHITE SOX????

Written by the Social Theatre™ Fall 2016 Jr. High Group

CHARACTERS

- ✓ White Sox fan (Buzz Kill)
- ✓ Cubs fans
- ✓ Cubs fan #1
- ✓ Cubs fan #2
- ✓ Narrator/Cubs fan #3

At a Cubs championship party, Cubs fans are watching the game on TV.

Cubs fans: Go! GO GO GO GO!

Cubs fan #1: I hope they win!

Cubs fan #2: Only one more run to go! NO outs, no outs!

Cubs fan #3: Ooooo! That was CL-OSE!

The Cubs fans stare intently at the TV, showing suspenseful feelings—on the edge of their seats, grasping with their hands on the edge of the chairs/sofa, leaning in...

White Sox fan: Hey guys!

Cubs fans: Hi! [*Looking away fast and focusing back on the game, not making eye contact.*]

Cubs fan #1: [*Watching game, but pulling a seat over while watching the game.*] Have a seat, watch with us.

White Sox fan: UGH...NO! I don't want to watch the Cubs. I hope they lose. GO WHITE SOX!!! GO WHITE SOX!

Cubs fan #2: If you don't like the Cubs, what brought you here?

The Cubs fans pause, looking annoyed and uncomfortable.

Narrator: FREEZE! What is going on here?

How do the Cubs fans feel? What happened that made the Cubs fans uncomfortable? Was the White Sox fan thinking about the Cubs fans' feelings?

The narrator wakes up the White Sox fan. The others stay frozen.

Narrator: I think you forgot to think about your friends, how they feel, and what they are doing. Look at them. Where are they? Who are they looking at? What are they feeling? If you think of all of these things together, you will figure out what to do next.

White Sox fan: [*Looks at Cubs game on TV, then looks at his friends looking at him annoyed, and looks at his White Sox hat.*] Yeah... I now see my friends are annoyed. They are looking at me and totally annoyed with me... Did I just kill their moment? Uh oh, I need to do something to make it better.

Narrator: Good idea. Try it! Unfreeze!

The Cubs fans look annoyed and are uncomfortably looking at each other and the White Sox fan.

White Sox fan: I'm sorry, guys. I didn't want to be a buzz kill. I can see now how exciting it is to be a Cubs fan right now. You guys are SO excited about this game!!! So, can I join you?

All Cubs fans: Yes!!!

The group cheers for the last few minutes of the game, and the Cubs win.

Cubs fans and White Sox fan: [*Stand up, cheering.*] YES!!! [*The friends cheer, getting into a circle, holding each other's shoulders, and jump around in a circle yelling.*] THEY WON! THEY WON!!! [*Then, high fiving each other.*]

THAT MAGIC ISN'T REAL!!!

Written by the Sahs Comedy Improv Troupe
(School Social Theatre™), November 2016

CHARACTERS

- √ Magician
- √ Buzz Kill
- √ Narrator
- √ Kids
- √ Mom/Dad

Magician: [*Does silly magic tricks that are obvious. Throws a ball then shows everyone the bucket is empty.*] See? Look at that! Empty bucket! [*Shows everyone empty coloring book pages.*] Look at my coloring book. There is no color on these pages.

[*Takes markers, turns around and scribbles on a page, puts markers in a book. Opens book to scribbled-on pages to show everyone the magic coloring book.*]

Magician: See? Magic! There's scribble on these pages!

The kids are cheering and are very excited.

Buzz Kill: Come on, can't you see it's fake?

Narrator: Freeze! [*Looks at audience.*] How did the kids feel when Buzz Kill said the magic trick was fake—even though it was?

How did the magician feel?

If you walk into a room where everyone is excited and no one is getting hurt, what would you do?

Unfreeze and rewind!

Magician: [*Doing silly magic tricks and throws the ball from the bucket, shows everyone it's empty.*] See? Look at that! Empty bucket!

The kids cheer.

Buzz Kill: [*Looks around awkwardly, surprised that others believe, but sits down and remains quiet.*]

Mom or Dad: It's time for pizza!

And then the group leaves the stage to eat pizza.

Chapter Five

PRACTICING RECOGNITION OF SOCIAL CUES

Increasingly, research has focused on eye gaze and social cognition (Marotta *et al.* 2013; Tipples, Johnston and Mayes 2013). A research study (Marotta *et al.* 2013) focused on analyzing eye gaze differences in those with autism and those without. Differences showed a slower reaction time to visual cues as well as peripheral cues in those with autism. This research supports a growing body of evidence regarding spectrum disorders, difficulty with eye gaze and inhibition of return, which is the accuracy and speed at which an object or cue is recognized. The difficulty of being able to recognize social cues due to visual speed often presents itself in real time, so interventions are needed to address recognizing social cues in real time.

Moreover, many of our clients and students struggle with recognizing the timings of social interaction, as well as recognizing cues from others and how others are reacting to their interactions. Theory of mind (Premack and Woodruff 1978) is important in recognizing facial expression, as well as noting what activities and materials are present in the environment and eye gaze direction in order to put together the puzzle pieces of social situations.

In Social Thinking® methodology, Michelle Garcia Winner discusses the importance of "detective skills": of using our "eyes, ears, and brain" to understand what to do next. In detail, this means to look with one's eyes to see how others are feeling, look at cues in the environment and the setting, and look at what people are doing. With our ears, it's important to listen to voice levels, the words of others, and other noise around us. With this information gathered in our brains, we can then process it along with what type of behavior is "expected," and utilize our filters to respond in an "expected" manner. In this chapter, activities are focused on recognizing social skills, which are referred to as "detective skills" and using the "Social Formula," which is discussed in a Social Thinking® children's book called *You Are a Social Detective* (Winner and Crooke 2008).

When performing on stage, participants must be aware of each other in relation to space as well as body expression. Using differences in body expression can make performances fun and multi-dimensional, whereas performers who only stand side by side are one-dimensional and boring. In order to create visual appeal, theatre participants must observe others and recognize their body expression and space in order to react with their own bodies.

USING STAGE LEVELS

In this activity we define how we are using our body in the stage space and practice understanding of how others are using space, and being able to react to others' body expression.

Teach and practice stage levels together:

Level 5: Hands up in the air, jumping, or standing elevated on something.

Level 4: Standing with arms lower than shoulder level.

Level 3: Crouching, squatting, or sitting in a chair.

Level 2: Knees on the floor or sitting on the floor.

Level 1: Lying on back or stomach.

Next, say "Ready, set, freeze." On the word "freeze," participants will choose a pose of differing levels. Look at the poses and note if they were able to reflect different levels and if the group was able to show all five levels. Repeat as many times as the group wants, then change to a different activity.

CONVERSATIONAL RECIPROCITY IMPROVISATIONAL GAME

Average exchanges in conversation are 1680 milliseconds, which converts to 1.68 seconds (Levinson and Torreira 2015). Furthermore, 95 percent of conversation is defined by one person talking at a time, whereas only 3.8 percent includes overlap, when two or more people talk at the same time.

Before playing this game, explain the meaning of conversational reciprocity. Then, explain that the typical response should be 1.68 seconds or less (Levinson and Torreira 2015). However, some wiggle room should be given because 1.68 seconds is not a lot of time for those who may have communication difficulties. Therefore, each participant can have 30 seconds to summarize their idea and then the participant must pass the turn to the next person.

The group tells a story together by being able to summarize their piece of the story in 5 seconds or less. Have the group sit in a circle, and utilize a timer for 5 seconds for each turn. The ultimate goal is to have participants tell a story that makes sense. Have players go in order.

Challenge: Group members can pick each other out of order using verbal communication and gestures.

Next challenge: Group members can pick each other with only gestures.

Next challenge: Group members can pick each other with only their eyes and facial expression.

PRACTICING AND UNDERSTANDING "AWKWARD"

When working with the participants in group, I have found those who struggle with social skills to have difficulty recognizing when others feel awkward. Awkward feelings can be subtle and difficult to recognize, since much of the time people are also trying to be nice. Therefore, before teaching this skit, have the participants brainstorm a list of body and facial expressions that demonstrate the feeling of "awkward." If they have difficulty discussing a list, then they can first practice what awkward and uncomfortable looks like, then the list can be made by looking at each other and identifying the body and facial expressions.

Your list might contain some of the following:

- a side glance

- a tilt of the head to the side

- chin tilted down, peering at person upwards

- body turning away

- looking away from the person they feel awkward about

- sighing

- tilt of the shoulders

- raised eyebrows.

After making the list, have the participants demonstrate their feeling of awkward; maintain this look, and look at others' feelings of awkward. If the group members are comfortable with each other, they will understand that awkward feelings can be pointed out in order to help each other and process if needed.

Next, have your group brainstorm and collaborate on two topics:

- A topic the group would want to talk about.

- A very random topic the group (and most people in the world) would not want to talk about.

The stranger the idea, the better. This is why the original Social Theatre™ group chose the topic of chairs as our "random topic." Ideas of other random topics could be: Kleenex, nail clippings, dandruff, crumbs on the floor, and what has been found between your toes. Also, rambling on and on about facts about anything without allowing someone to contribute can be quite awkward too, which would also make a great "random" topic.

QUESTION–COMMENT FORMAT FROM SUPERFLEX CURRICULUM®

The whole-group discussion is a great time to practice the "question–comment" Social Thinking® strategy from *Superflex Takes on One-Sided Sid, Un-Wonderer and the Team of Unthinkables* (Winner and Madrigal 2013). The question–comment format is used during conversation to help participants remember to make a comment, then ask a question to others afterwards.

For the purposes of the following skit, question–comment format may be utilized in a line, just to get used to the format. If the group is larger than four or if the group members have difficulty with turn taking in conversation, the group can start with the person on the right and have them ask the person on their left a question, who answers with a comment, then continues the conversation by asking the next person on their left a question, continuing through the entire line. This strategy is also very important for the upcoming skit: "Chairs!!!"

And, of course, as participants become used to the question–comment format in a line, challenges can be added by breaking the participants into groups of two, then increasing the numbers in groups until the entire group can have a back and forth conversation by using the question–comment format.

TEACH THE SKILL OF ENTERING A GROUP

After teaching the first part of the play and the narrator script for "Chairs!!!", teach participants how to enter a group. Here are the standard steps in entering a group:

1. Looking at the group, decide who is typically welcoming.

2. Walk up slowly to the group and match the others' levels of energy.

3. Stand next to someone typically welcoming.

4. Smile, look at those talking, and listen to the group discussion.

5. Once there is a break in conversation, add an idea or comment.

CHAIRS!!!

Written by the Sahs Comedy Improv Troupe in 2015

CHARACTERS

- √ Actor who talks off-topic and babbles
- √ Narrator
- √ Those who are already involved in a conversation

One participant is waiting backstage while the rest of the group members are discussing a mutually agreed upon topic. Example: planning a birthday party in Hawaii. After all of the participants have had a chance to ask a question and make a comment to each other, the participant waiting backstage comes out on stage.

The participant coming out on stage begins talking about the "random topic" that all have agreed not many would want to talk about. This actor is talking rapidly, with too many details, and is not noticing the awkward, bored, and uncomfortable expressions and body language from others in the group.

> Narrator: FREEZE!
>
> What is going on here?
>
> What are they talking about?
>
> What are the kids' faces telling you? What are their bodies telling you?
>
> How is the kid feeling, who is talking about chairs [or other off-topic subject]?

The narrator unfreezes the actor who is discussing chairs—or another off-topic subject.

> Narrator: How do you think you should enter a group?
>
> That's right. Stand next to them first to find out what they are talking about, then make a comment.
>
> UNFREEZE!

The participant who comes out on stage will show the correct way to join the group.

Discussion about the collaborated topic begins again and an audience member (or the theatre participant interested in chairs) shows how to enter the group.

The following skit is from the Sahs Comedy Improv Troupe's skit about not "using one's eyes" and "tools" in order to figure out a social situation. This skit discusses the use of the Social Formula, from *You*

Are a Social Detective (Winner and Crooke 2008) in order to figure out a situation.

WHY DID YOU DO THAT?

Written by the Sahs Comedy Improv Troupe, 2016–17

CHARACTERS

- √ Basketball player, who gets blamed
- √ Basketball player in Defence, who gets hit with a broom
- √ Janitor
- √ Narrator

Two friends are playing basketball in a gymnasium. They stop to discuss strategy about the game.

The janitor is sweeping in a very excited fashion, while listening to music. The janitor is walking close to the basketball players and while sweeping, accidentally hits one of the players with the broom.

The basketball player who was hit: [*Says to the other basketball player*] Why did you do that?!

Narrator: FREEZE!

What is going on in this scene?

What was expected? What was unexpected?

What did the basketball player think? Did the basketball player use his "tools"?

Have other participants who are not currently in the play hold the "Social Formula" visual.

Narrator: Did the basketball player use his eyes? What happened that makes you think this?

Was the basketball player using his tools, his eyes, to know who hit him? If he was, what would he have seen?

Was the janitor using his tools: his eyes? If he had been, what would he have seen? Was the janitor using his ears? If he had been, what might he have heard?

What was expected of the janitor? What was expected of the basketball player? How could he have prevented this? Okay, let's try it.

The narrator walks to the basketball player who blamed, unfreezes the basketball player, and teaches them the "Social Formula."

Narrator: UNFREEZE, REWIND!

The scene starts over.

The basketball players are in a gym, the janitor accidentally hits one of the players with the broom. The player who was hit "uses his tools: his eyes" by looking around to see what and who could have hit him. He looks at the janitor with the broom.

Janitor: [*Reciprocates eye contact and says*] Sorry, I was so involved in sweeping; I will use my eyes to look around next time.

Basketball player: That's okay. Thanks!

The basketball players go back to shooting hoops.

The janitor goes back to sweeping.

The following is a skit we wrote in our Spring Social Theatre™ group in 2016. The purpose of this play was to identify ineffective and effective ways to ask others to hang out. The last way is the effective way to ask others to hang out.

WANNA HANG OUT?

Written by the 2016 Spring Social Theatre™ group

(Five ways to invite someone to spend time with you)

CHARACTERS

√   Mr./Ms. Oliver—teacher/narrator
√   Simon—student
√   Colleen—student
√   Bethany—student

Mr./Ms. Oliver: Today we will have a science test. Here are your tests. [*Passing out paper.*] Good luck.

During a science test...

Simon: Hey guys! Do you want to hang out on Saturday?

Colleen and Bethany: [*Look at Simon with awkward, uncomfortable look.*]

Colleen: [*Whisper*] Shhhh!!!

Bethany: [*Whisper*] It's a science test!

Mr./Ms. Oliver: FREEZE! Is this the right time to ask someone to hang out? Unfreeze Simon. It's important to ask at the right time: during a test or class is definitely not the right time. UNFREEZE and try again!

Simon: [*Walking in the hallway*] Hey guys! Let's get together!

Colleen: Sure.

Bethany: Okay.

Simon: [*Walks away.*]

Mr./Ms. Oliver: FREEZE! I think he forgot to discuss details. They didn't know when or where he wanted to hang out. Unfreeze Simon. Simon, try telling them where and when you want to hang out. That will help. UNFREEZE!

Walking in the hallway

Simon: [*Using no eye contact.*] Hey guys! Want to hang out at the park after school?

Colleen: Is he talking to us?

Bethany: Simon, who are you talking to?

Mr./Ms. Oliver: FREEZE! Simon did give them details on where and when to hang out, but they didn't know he was talking to them because he wasn't looking at them. Unfreeze Simon. Simon, try looking in their eyes when you talk to them. UNFREEZE!

Colleen and Bethany: [*Pretending to be talking in the hallway at their lockers.*]

Simon: [*Walks down off of the stage and looks at someone he does not know.*] Hi! Would you like to hang out at the park after this?

Mr./Ms. Oliver: FREEZE!!!! It's really important to know someone on a friend level before asking them to hang out. Unfreeze Simon. If we aren't friends with a person, it would make them feel uncomfortable if we invite them to hang out. Who are you friends with? Who do you have a conversation with at least every day?

Simon: I'm friends with Colleen and Bethany.

Mr./Ms. Oliver: Okay, there you go. Try it! UNFREEZE!!

Colleen and Bethany: [*Walking slowly, talking in the hall.*]

Simon: [*Walks up and joins Colleen and Bethany walking. All stop to talk.*] Hey guys! What are you up to after school? Want to go to the park?

Colleen: Yeah! That will be fun!

Bethany: I'm in too. Just have to text my mom.

Colleen: Oh yeah, me too.

Simon: Me three!

MATCH THE FEELINGS (PAIRS WITH "STOP CHASING ME!")

Have two cards for each feeling, and just enough cards for the number of participants in the group. Have each person take a card. Explain that they need to walk around quietly, demonstrating the feeling and stand next to the other person they think has the matching feeling.

- How did you know your feelings were matching?

- What is important about having matching feelings?

- What might happen if people do not have matching feelings in a situation?

- What would you do if your feeling about the same situation did not match (e.g. if someone was chasing you and your feeling did not match theirs)?

The following skit is about unmatching feelings during an uncommunicated game of chase. We turned this into a skit about using Winner and Crooke's Social Thinking® Social Formula from their book, *You Are a Social Detective* (2008).

STOP CHASING ME!

Written by Social Theatre™ fall session, 2015

CHARACTERS

- √   Mr./Mrs. Oliver—teacher narrator
- √   Colleen—student
- √   Simon—student
- √   Bethany—student

Colleen and Bethany are talking at the playground.

Colleen: Oh! Wait. I have to go ask the teacher something. I'll be back.

Bethany: That's okay. I want to go play tag.

Colleen goes up to the teacher (Mr. Oliver) and is talking to him.

Bethany chases Simon (background chase music: "Yakety Sax," Randolph and Rich 1963).

Simon: [*Does not look happy as he's running.*] Stop chasing me! Stop!

Mr./Ms. Oliver: Bethany, he's asking you to stop! You will get a detention.

Mr./Ms. Oliver: FREEZE!

What is going on here?

What is he [*pointing to Simon*] feeling?

What is she [*pointing to Bethany*] feeling?

Do their feelings match?

Unfreeze Bethany only. Bethany, it's important that we use our eyes to notice how others are feeling. [*Gives her eyeglasses and waits until she puts them on.*] It's also important to use our ears to notice what others are saying and their tone of voice. [*Gives her ears and waits until she puts them on.*] Then, it's important to use our brains to figure out if our behavior is unexpected or expected. [*Gives her brain hat and waits until she puts it on.*] If we do this, it will be easy to know what to do next.

Unfreeze and rewind!

Colleen and Bethany are talking.

Colleen: Oh! Wait. I have to go tell my friend something. I'll be back.

Bethany: That's okay. I want to go play tag. Hey, Simon! Wait up. Do you want to play tag?

Simon: Sure, Bethany! Let's ask Colleen too. Hey, Colleen, want to play tag?

Colleen, Bethany, and Simon are playing tag.

Mr./Ms. Oliver: Recess is over! Everyone get in line. I am so proud of you guys! I really like it when my students follow directions and get along so well.

FEELINGS RECOGNITION SEQUENCE

The following skit includes a behavioral rehearsal sequence of stopping to look how someone feels and thinking what to do next. The main idea of this skit is that acting silly does not always help others who are feeling alone to feel happy and comfortable, but inviting someone to spend actual time together can help someone feel less lonely. A discussion can be held afterwards to discuss how people sometimes try to relate to each other only by making jokes and miss getting to know people for who they are.

CALL ME WHEN YOU'RE DOWN

Written by the Sahs Comedy Improv Troupe, 2003, and altered in 2016

One actor sits in the middle of the stage, lonely and sad. Music from Le Clic "Call Me" (1997) is playing.

The rest of the groups splits in two, one group on stage right behind the curtain, and the other group on stage left, behind the curtain.

When the beat starts, one actor from stage left skips onto the stage and carries out the following sequence.

The actor skips on stage, acts shocked when seeing the sad and lonely character. Then, the actor starts thinking about how they can make the sad/lonely actor/actress happy. Then, the actor makes the idea sign with their finger. The actor/actress tries to make the sad/lonely actor laugh by doing something funny. When the sad/lonely actor doesn't laugh, the actor/actress shrugs and skips off the stage.

This first part of the sequence is behavioral rehearsal of how to recognize feelings.

PAUSE, NOTICE!

Hmmm... Think.

IDEA!

The rest of the sequence.

Try something silly, it doesn't work.

Shrug.

Walk away.

The next actor/actress from stage right skips onto the stage, repeats the pattern, skips off the stage, and repeats from stage left. Continue this sequence with the rest of the actors—stage right zthen stage left—until only one actor is left behind the stage curtains.

After all but one actor/actress has tried unsuccessfully to make the sad actor/actress laugh, the last actor/actress skips out on stage, repeats the same pattern, except they invite all of the others to come up on stage and waves them into a huddle. They whisper and look at the sad actor/actress, and then one of the actors holds up their finger to symbolize an "idea." The actor waves all of the others over to the sad actor/actress and holds out his hand to stand up, and others gesture to the sad actor/actress to come with them. The sad actor/actress and others in the group can do a quick hand slapping game or do a fancy handshake while directing HUGE smiles at each other. Then—with the sad actor/actress now being incredibly happy and being part of the group—walking off stage.

The lesson is that the sad actor/actress is lonely. Being lonely won't be solved by someone just trying to make them laugh. It is solved by having others truly include and invite them to be together with their peers.

- What was the actor/actress sitting in the middle of the stage feeling? (*Sad, lonely, depressed.*)

- What was happening to try to cheer them up? (*Trying to make them laugh.*) Did it work?

- Why didn't it work? (*They were actually lonely and wanted to be included.*)

- What is involved with trying to be friends? What do people sometimes forget when they are trying so hard to make each other laugh? (*They forget to get to know people by asking questions.*)

- What does it mean to have a friend only on the surface? (*Friends who might make each other laugh, but not know anything deeper and don't know what else to talk about, which still can cause loneliness.*)

BY ACCIDENT OR ON PURPOSE?

Brainstorm things that can be on purpose, and have the group identify the alternative "by accident" in each situation. Write "on purpose" examples on paper and have participants act out each incident; have others identify if by accident or on purpose. Then, have the group act out the alternative. Discuss why it appears to be by accident or on purpose.

For example, the lists might say:

By accident

Person not looking at them before.

The person may not have realized it happened.

No eye contact.

No mischievous look.

Did the situation occur in a tight space? Was the environment conducive to an accident possibly occurring?

Maybe the person apologized or looked uncomfortable.

On purpose

Was the person looking at them when they did it?

Did the person smile or have a mischievous look?

Did the person look like they were seeking approval from friends?

Practice a mischievous look.

BY ACCIDENT OR ON PURPOSE?

Written by the Sahs Improv Comedy Troupe, 2017 (School Social Theatre™ Program)

CHARACTERS

- √ Student who gets bumped
- √ Student who bumps
- √ Teacher
- √ Narrator
- √ Student who dabs
- √ Student who gets dabbed
- √ Others in line/others in dance party

Scene I

Students are standing in line in class, waiting for the end of the day bell to ring.

Teacher: Line up! The bell is going to ring. It's almost time to go to the afterschool dance party!

Student who bumps: [*While walking, student is reading and not paying attention. They walk and bump right into people who are in line.*]

Narrator: FREEZE!

What is going on here?

Was this on accident or on purpose?

How can you tell?

(The person who bumped into others was not even looking, but were absorbed in their book.)

Narrator: UNFREEZE!

Teacher: Line up! The bell is going to ring. It's almost time to go to the afterschool dance party!

Student who bumps: [*While walking toward the line, student bumps the last student in line on purpose.*]

Narrator: FREEZE!

What is going on here?

Was this by accident or on purpose?

How can you tell?

(The student looked at the person he bumped into first, had a "smirk," then bumped and laughed.)

Narrator: UNFREEZE!

(Students walk off stage.)

Scene II

Students walk back on stage where there is an afterschool dance.

The students put their backpacks by the wall and are dancing together.

Dabber: [*Not paying attention and dabbing while dancing, whacks another student in the face.*]

Narrator: FREEZE!

What is going on here?

Was this by accident or on purpose?

How can you tell?

(The person who dabbed was just dancing and dabbing, but didn't look to see if anyone was behind him/her.)

Narrator: UNFREEZE!

The students are dancing together.

Dabber: Hey guys! [*Looking at their peers and getting their attention to watch.*] Watch this!

Other students: [*Respond by watching dabber.*]

Dabber: [*Looks at another student dancing, dabs and purposely whacks the other student in the face.*]

Other students: [*Look shocked and upset.*]

Narrator: FREEZE!

What is going on here?

Was this by accident or on purpose?

How can you tell?

(The student gets peers' attention, plans in advance, looks at classmate before dabbing and whacking them in the face.)

Narrator: UNFREEZE!!

Other students: Why did you do that? That's mean!!

Dabber: [*Looks guilty, and thinks about what they did.*]

Dabber: I'm really sorry... I was trying to be funny, but I'm realizing it really wasn't funny. [*Says to dabbed student and others*] Let's dance!

Option: Have each actor/actress leave the stage and pick one younger child to come up on stage and continue the dance party for the rest of the song. Students can initiate the conga line or go down the line showing everyone doing that dance move.

Chapter Six

PRACTICING SELF-REGULATION SKILLS

This chapter on self-regulation skills is based upon cognitive behavioral theory (CBT), as well as emotion regulation. Feelings recognition, feelings levels, identifying feelings versus actions, identifying different problems and appropriate reactions, identifying and practicing voice levels are all activities that participants can practice to regulate and recognize feelings. Social skills behavioral rehearsal opportunities are presented in "The Missing Bunny," "Big Problem or Little Problem," and "Chain Reaction."

"EMOTIONAL COPING" EXERCISES

The skill of feelings recognition is important on so many different levels. In order to self-regulate, we must understand our own feelings and coping skills. In order to participate socially, we must be able to recognize the feelings of others, and be able to connect this with the environmental cues of what is happening around us. In order to practice feelings recognition, we have included some exercises that demonstrate feelings recognition.

FEELINGS CHARADES

For this game, some of the feelings pictures from the book *The Zones of Regulation®* (Kuypers 2011) are helpful because the feelings faces are realistic, which can help participants generalize feelings recognition skills to other social situations.

Utilize feelings pictures as visual cards, placing them face down on the table. The first player should blindly pick a card, which they then demonstrate. If others are having difficulty guessing the feeling, if the player with the card has the ability, they could discuss what makes someone feel that way. If the player needs help, they can pick someone to help. After someone guesses the correct feeling, the next player can choose a card.

LEVELS OF EMOTIONS

Students can practice naming their level of emotions on a five-point rating scale by practicing these emotions. For example, a level 5 scared would be absolutely terrified, and a level 1 scared would be a little nervous. Practice these emotions together and look around to notice how others might express their different levels of emotions.

After this activity, questions to ask include:

- Why did we practice feelings levels?

- Why are feelings levels important on stage?

- Why are feelings levels important off stage?

- Did you notice that anyone expressed a feeling differently than you? How so?

- In what situations might it be okay to express a scared feeling at level 5? Or a happy feeling at level 5 (or mad level 2, sad level 2, or other feelings/levels)?

FEELING OR ACTION?

Print out the "Feeling or Action" cards from Appendix B. Have a participant pick a card and demonstrate the action or feeling. Then, have group members identify if it's a feeling or an action.

After this activity, questions can be asked, such as:

- Why do you think we just did this activity?

- Why is it important to tell the difference between feelings and actions?

- What happens when someone thinks a feeling and action are the same? (e.g. Teacher asks "How did you feel about that?" Student replies "Well... I hit him.")

- Why would this be a problem? (*Because we must be able to identify our feelings first in order to have access to coping skills.*)

VOICE LEVELS ACTIVITY

Many do not understand or pay attention to their voice levels. Moreover, when a child is angry and needs to express anger, the reaction of screaming sometimes follows. In this activity, participants learn voice levels as well as practice expressing anger with a medium voice.

Participants practice voice levels starting at a whisper level 1 up to a screaming level 5. Then the group learns to say a phrase they would most likely say in a raised tone of voice, in a calmer level 3 tone of voice. A few volunteers are asked to say it at a level 3 first, and discuss how saying it this way feels. Then the group practices chanting together "It's not my fault, it's your fault" at a level 3. This is an extremely difficult feat, and helps participants practice self-control with voice level and emotions. For an added challenge and to add visual interest during the play, have participants chant together "It's not my fault, it's your fault" in a level 3 tone but also point in different places with both pointer fingers.

Questions after this activity:

- How did this activity make you feel?

- Who felt this was a challenge? Why? (*Polar opposite: communication of emotionally charged words in a level 3 voice.*)

- Why did we do this activity?

- What do you think it teaches?

UNDERSTANDING, TEACHING, AND DISCUSSING COGNITIVE DISTORTIONS

Before teaching "The Missing Bunny," we need to teach a few common cognitive distortions, including blaming.

Burns (1989) labeled different types of thinking errors in his book, *The Feeling Good Handbook: Using the New Mood Therapy in Everyday Life*. All of the cognitive distortions listed can create anxiety or depression, unless thinking distortions are changed. In teaching this skit, it might be helpful to go over some of the common thinking errors that people have.

1. "All or Nothing Thinking": Thinking things are black and white, either perfect or very bad.

2. "Overgeneralization": Taking a single event and seeing it as a recurring pattern.

3. "Mental Filter": Only selecting a negative detail, and continuously thinking about the negative detail until your perception of reality is altered to a darker way of seeing things.

4. "Disqualifying the Positive": Paying attention to negative experiences, and weeding out all positive experiences information that would not support the negative evidence.

5. "Jumping to Conclusions": You interpret something in a certain way, but there is no clear evidence to support your interpretation.

   i.   "Mind Reading": You think someone has acted a certain way because of you, but there is no evidence to support this or you have not asked them.

   ii. "Fortune Telling": Before something even happens, you strongly predict a specific outcome.

6. "Magnification or Minimization": When a problem occurs, you feel the problem is much larger than it actually is. In minimization, you feel the problem is much smaller than it actually is and might state it is "not a big deal" (see "Big Problem or Little Problem").

7. "Emotional Reasoning": The belief that your own thoughts or others' statements must be true. For example, she said I'm a loser, so I'm a loser. I had a thought that I'm stupid, so I must be stupid.

8. "Shoulds, Coulds, Woulds": "Should," "could," "would," and "if only" statements are when you overanalyze what you did in the past and what you should do in the future. This also applies to how you might think you or others should act. When things aren't done in the way you think they should be done, the end result is frustration and anger.

9. "Labeling": Labeling is more intense than generalization, and is when you actually label misbehavior or deviations by name calling or with other negative labels.

10. "Personalization" (Blaming): Blaming yourself or others for something that was not actually your/their fault.

THE MISSING BUNNY

Written by the Sahs Comedy Improv Troupe in 2008

CHARACTERS

√ Magician
√ Actors (a flexible number)
√ Narrator

PROPS

√ Toy bunny
√ Decorative box

Magician: Do do dah do do dah. Zip-a-dee doodah! [*Holding bunny.*] I LOVE my bunny! He loves to hop hop hop [*hopping*]. What's that? [*Holds bunny next to ear.*] Really? Are you telling me you want to do what? You want to hide? Okay. Hmmmm... Where could you hide? [*Looking around.*] Say what? You can hide where? Ooooohhhhh! You want to hide in there? The BOX?! Well... Okay. I'll put you in the box. Okay. See you later!

The magician walks off stage.

Actors walk across the stage, show time change—going for a walk. Picking flowers. Practicing Tai Chi in the park. Other actors yawn, show they are tired and ready to go home, stretch and walk off the stage.

Magician: Oh my gosh! I forgot to look for bunny! I don't know where he went! I'll try the box—he's not in here, it's empty! [*Taking lots of time showing the audience the empty box. Then getting really mad.*] I know! I know who TOOK my bunny! _____(name) took my bunny.

(Actor 1)   I didn't take your bunny, Actor 2 took your bunny.

(Actor 2)   I didn't take your bunny, Actor 3 took your bunny.

(Actor 3)   I didn't take your bunny, Actor 4 took your bunny.

(Actor 4)   I didn't take your bunny, Actor 5 took your bunny.

(Actor 5)   I didn't take your bunny, Actor 6 took your bunny.

(Actor 6)   I didn't take your bunny, Actor 7 took your bunny.

(Actor 7)   I didn't take your bunny, Actor 8 took your bunny.

(Actor 8)   I didn't take your bunny, Actor 9 took your bunny.

Everyone else comes out on stage, starts pointing and repeating in unison level 3 loud and using all stage presence levels.

Actors: It's not my fault, it's your fault!

Narrator: FREEZE!

What is going on here?

What is the magician thinking? What is the magician feeling? What did he do wrong?

How are the friends feeling?

What might happen next?

What solutions could they use to resolve the problem?

UNFREEZE, REWIND!

Magician: Dooo doo dah! Zip-a-dee doodah, zip-a-dee eh. My oh my, what a wonderful day! Okay, so I still have to look for my bunny. He's lost. What should I do? What? Audience! What should I do? Oh! Are you saying I should try the HOCUS POCUS magic? Maybe that will help my bunny come back! Okay...let's try it together. Narrator! I need you!

The narrator comes out with a poster that says *"Hocus Pocus, Let's Focus, Take a Deep Breath and Relax."* Everyone else follows and watches from the back, showing interest, shrugging at each other.

Narrator and Magician: HOCUS POCUS

LET'S FOCUS

TAKE A DEEP BREATH

AND RELAX!

Narrator: [*To the audience*] I don't think it worked. You forgot to take a breath!

With the audience.

Narrator and Magician: HOCUS POCUS

LET'S FOCUS

TAKE A DEEP BREATH

AND RELAX!

Magician: [*Opens box*] OMG! It worked! Thank you audience! Thank you! Thank you! [*Then, dreadful silence, magician looks down, looks up at friends, then down again—embarrassed.*] UGH! Ugh. I blamed you! I am sooo sorry!

Actors: That's okay. Please don't blame us again. Next time just use the Hocus Pocus magic.

Everyone walks in a group, arm in arm, smiling, laughing, walking off the stage.

In this skit, blaming is discussed, how it can be passed on, and how it affects others' thoughts and feelings. Moreover, coping skills are introduced as a replacement for blaming.

BEING FLEXIBLE

Scott (1962) coined the term "cognitive flexibility," which is the degree to which a person's ideas and beliefs can be changed when presented with more information. In a group, it is important to be accepting and flexible according to the information and ideas that others present, as a way to make sure others feel comfortable and as equal members of the group. For those who struggle with social-cognitive deficits and social skills, this can be a difficult feat. This skit demonstrates how one must be able to be flexible when plans change.

THE SMALL CHANGE

Written by the Social Theatre™ spring session, 2017

CHARACTERS

- √ Dave
- √ Dave's mom
- √ Billy
- √ Narrator

Narrator: One day there were two friends, Billy and Dave. They were at school, packing up for the end of the school day.

Dave: Billy, are you still coming over to my house after school?

Billy: Yes! I can't wait!

Dave: I'm just dialing my mom to make sure she knows we are on our way home. [*Pause as he dials phone.*] Mom? Hi. Billy and I are walking home from school now.

Dave's Mom: [*On other side of stage, back to Dave and Billy.*] Yes, I am expecting both of you home soon. Billy's mom called and he actually has to go to golf practice. His mom asked us to drop him off there.

Dave: WHAT! I PLANNED EVERYTHING OUT AND THIS IS WHAT I GET?! NOT FAIR! NOT FAIR! Once we finally plan and get to play together, now we have to drive him to golf practice? What happened to me getting to play with my friend? That's SO WRONG, Mom! [*Tantrum type of behavior, throws down backpack, yelling, etc.*]

Billy: [*Feeling awkward, looking at Dave, not knowing what to say.*]

Narrator: FREEZE!

What's going on here?

What does Dave's Mom feel? What does Billy feel?

Is this a small problem or just a little change? Correct! This is a little change and a small problem. Dave should try to be flexible and relax so he can problem solve.

What can Dave do?

GREAT idea! Let's see what Dave will do! UNFREEZE!

Dave: I'm so sorry I overreacted, I'll reschedule. Billy and I can hang out another day.

Dave's Mom: That sounds good. See you when you get home.

Dave and Billy are still walking home.

Dave: Let's hang out this Saturday.

Billy: Okay!

Billy and Dave arrive at Dave's house, go in, and say hi to Dave's Mom.

Dave: Hi Mom!

Billy: Hi Mrs. Schmave!

Dave's Mom: Hi! Are you guys ready? Billy, we have to get you to golf practice!

They all walk off stage together.

MAGNIFICATION AND MINIMIZATION

"Magnification" and "minimization" are seen as cognitive distortions according to cognitive behavioral theory as discussed in *The Feeling Good Handbook* by Burns (1989). Social Thinking® introduces magnification and minimization through the concept "size of the problem." "Size of the problem" is a familiar concept introduced in Social Thinking® methodology and is explained in many of Michelle Garcia Winner's books. Two chapters explain it in kid-friendly language in the two-book set, *Social Thinking® and Me*, by Michelle Garcia Winner and Linda Murphy (2016). Book 1 (*Kids' Guidebook to Social Emotional Learning*) is a colorfully illustrated book that talks directly to kids, and book 2 (*Thinksheets for Social Emotional Learning*) gives kids tons of practice in using the concept. This concept helps kids better understand that problems come in different sizes and it's expected when in social situations that our reactions should match the size of the problem.

MATCHING REACTIONS IMPROV

An activity we practice before trying the script "Big Problem or Little Problem" is to brainstorm different sized problems and different sized reactions. We mix and match problems and reactions to make appropriate scenarios and silly scenarios. Use Post-it® notes to have kids write down problems on pink pieces of paper, and reactions or solutions on yellow pieces of paper. Separate the paper into two piles, and have a person pick one from each pile, then act out the problem with the solution. This could also be the start of your own "Big Problem or Little Problem" skit!

- What were examples of the "size of a problem" matching a reaction?

- What were some examples of a problem that did not match a reaction?

- Why did these problems and reactions work? Or not work?

- How would others feel if the reactions worked? Or did not work?

Discuss that problems can be small and reactions can be big on stage, which makes for great comedy. However, discuss the difference between on stage and how people would feel about these examples in real life.

The Sahs Comedy Improv Troupe (School Social Theatre™ program) collaboratively wrote the skit "Big Problem or Little Problem?" which is about matching reactions to the size of a problem, the concept of "size of the problem" from Social Thinking®.

BIG PROBLEM OR LITTLE PROBLEM?

Written by the Sahs Comedy Improv Troupe, 2014–2015

Because participants are not supposed to memorize lines, these parts are variable. As long as participants know what is supposed to happen in a scene, they can help each other through.

CHARACTERS

- √ Student/hiker who falls off the cliff
- √ Other students/hikers who react
- √ Student who breaks a pencil
- √ Other students who react or help
- √ Narrator

(CONCEPT OF "SIZE OF THE PROBLEM" FROM MICHELLE GARCIA WINNER'S SOCIAL THINKING® METHODOLOGY)

The students walk on stage, setting the scene for being at the Grand Canyon. They decide their relationship to each other and can say relevant statements about the Grand Canyon to help the audience understand where they are.

(Differentiated learning: teach the meaning of "reflective statement" for those who are ready to practice the skill, and have them add reflective statements in between comments.)

Student 1: WOW! The Grand Canyon is AMAZING!

Student 2: I don't even want to look. That's a LONG way down.

Student 3: Look at the rock formations!

Student 4: There's even a river down there! I want to get a selfie.

Other students: [*Not reacting to the fact student 4 is getting too close to the edge.*]

Student 4 falls (jumps lightly) off the stage, doing a dramatic (and controlled) fall onto the auditorium floor (or a dramatic fall from a chair).

Dramatic pause without emotion.

Student 1: [*Walks over to the edge, then looks up at the audience.*] Hmph. [*Walks away.*]

Student 3: [*Waves to the others to come closer to the edge. Looks down at her nails as if she's looking down at the person who fell.*] Look! That's horrible! I need a manicure!

Narrator: FREEZE!

Big problem or little problem?

Big reaction or small reaction?

How did it make you feel that they had a small reaction? What KIND of reaction do you need to have to this type of BIG problem?

Let's rewind and try it the right way.

UNFREEZE and REWIND!

Student 1: WOW! The Grand Canyon is AMAZING!

Student 2: I don't even want to look. That's a LONG way down.

Student 3: Look at the rock formations!

Student 4: There's even a river down there! I want to get a selfie.

Other students: You are getting too close to the edge! Watch out!

Student 4 falls (jumps lightly) off the stage, doing a dramatic (and controlled) fall onto the auditorium floor (or a dramatic fall from a chair).

All students run to the edge, and panic.

Student 1: Oh! Oh! I don't know what to do! [*Crying hysterically.*]

Student 2: I see someone coming. I'm running to get help!

Student 3: Let's call 911!

All students run off the stage.

All students come back on stage with chairs. They sit their chairs in classroom formation. They have to set the scene by making statements and giving clues about where they are and what they are doing.

Student 1: [*Speaking clearly in a stage voice, loud enough to hear, but demonstrating a whisper.*] 4 + 5 equals...equals...9!

Student 2: [*Scratching head and counting on fingers. Erasing and writing.*]

Student 3: [*Raising hand.*] Ms. Teacher, can you help me? I don't understand this.

Student 4: [*Writing and starts looking at the tip of her pencil. Goes from calm to level 1, 2, 3, 4, 5 anger while looking at her pencil.*] Now I can't do my MATH WORK! My pencil BROKE!

All students run to student 4 and panic.

Student 1: Oh! Oh! I don't know what to do! [*Crying hysterically.*]

Student 2: I see someone coming. I'm running to get help!

Student 3: Let's call 911!

Narrator: FREEZE!

Big problem or little problem?

Big reaction or small reaction?

How did it make you feel that they had a BIG reaction? What KIND of reaction do you need to have in this type of small problem?

Let's rewind and try it the right way.

UNFREEZE and REWIND!

Student 1: [*Speaking clearly in a stage voice, loud enough to hear, but demonstrating a whisper.*] 4 + 5 equals...equals...9!

Student 2: [*Scratching head and counting on fingers. Erasing and writing.*]

Student 3: [*Raising hand.*] Ms. Teacher, can you help me? I don't understand this.

Student 4: [*Writing and starts looking at the tip of her pencil. While looking at her pencil, student looks in her desk, doesn't see another pencil. However, she quietly turns to her classmate.*] Can I borrow a pencil? [*Her classmate loans her a pencil and she goes back to work.*]

All students work for a bit. The students are calm, focused, quiet, and continue to do their work.

Narrator: [*Walks to the front center stage.*]

How did you feel about this reaction? We agreed it is a small problem. Did the reaction match the size of the problem? How does it make you feel when someone's reaction matches the size of the problem?

Have your students brainstorm small, medium, and big problems, as well as act out small, medium, and big reactions. The students can improvise their own skits with matched and mismatched reactions and problems.

CHAIN REACTION AND "PROJECTION"

Anger can be passed on just as easily as kindness. In this skit, students learn and teach others examples of how anger can be shared and easily changed to shared kindness. Sigmund and Anna Freud originally formed the defense mechanism meaning of projection, where someone has an angry feeling, then projects that feeling onto someone else with mean words (simplypsychology.org). The deeper meaning of the term projection is that someone actually believes deep down that they are what they are projecting onto someone else. For example, the big brother might call his sister a "loser," when in fact, he might feel like the one who is a loser. This concept should be taught to participants to help them understand what they will be practicing, and possibly performing.

In therapeutic settings: clients can process ways they put themselves down, which can include self-name calling. If clients can identify the specific names they call themselves, they can use this name to pass it to the next person during this exercise, since it is only acting. For those who self-name call, it might be an opportunity to be introspective and to say the name out loud, especially to another person. During the second half of the exercise, the client can think of what they would say to effectively apologize and therefore, also process that they can apologize to themselves.

CHAIN REACTION

Written by the Sahs Comedy Improv Troupe in 2006

CHARACTERS

- √ Big brother
- √ Big sister
- √ Little sister (or brother)
- √ Sister's friend
- √ Friend's friend
- √ Friend's brother
- √ Brother's classmate

Many other characters can also be added. The more quickly this is demonstrated and the more people there are in the line, the more powerful this representation is.

The big brother has a bad day at school.

He comes home and calls his big sister a name.

Then the big sister calls the little sister a name.

Then the little sister calls the sister's friend a name.

Then the sister's friend calls her friend a name.

Then the friend calls his (or her) brother a name.

Then the brother calls his classmate a name.

The classmate (last in line) then tells the big brother that someone called him a name.

> Narrator: FREEZE! What's going on here? That's right. Anger and frustration is like a chain reaction. Let's see what might happen next!

After the classmate told the big brother someone hurt his feelings.

> Big brother: If my friend's feelings got hurt, my sister's feelings were probably hurt too.

He then says sorry to the sister and pays her a compliment.

Then the big sister says sorry to the little sister and pays her a compliment.

Then the little sister says sorry to the sister's friend and pays her a compliment.

Then the sister's friend says sorry to her friend and pays him (or her) a compliment.

Then the friend says sorry to his brother and pays him a compliment.

Then the brother says sorry to his classmate and pays his classmate a compliment.

> Classmate: [*Smiles.*] I'm happy! [*Turns to everyone in line.*] Hey! We are all happy! Why don't we go do something together, it will be fun!

Everyone is now happy.

> Narrator: Do you see what happened? How did feelings change? It is possible to change someone's feelings, to positive or negative. You are right! Kindness is also like a chain reaction. What can change with kids your age? How can you help things change for the better?

Chapter Seven

PRACTICING PERSPECTIVE TAKING

Perspective taking is an important social skill, which tends to be a basis for empathy. Being in the education and helping fields, we can identify many who struggle with being able to understand others' perspectives. Perspective taking includes many different considerations, including self-judgement, projection, and comparison to others (Boven *et al.* 2005). In order for someone to have deeper perspective taking abilities, they must be able to remove themselves from comparing themself to the person who is in the situation, and truly see from a neutral aspect.

The activities in this chapter are designed as a way to help participants understand that there are different perspectives. In Seih and colleagues' (2011) study, it was found that when people write in the first person, perspective taking increases. Any situation can be created through writing or creating plays, establishing characters, and actually acting out a perspective that is not natural to oneself. This can help participants practice perspective taking skills.

USING MAGIC TO TEACH PERSPECTIVE TAKING

Teaching a child how to do a magic trick not only allows them to practice social skills, but can also teach them how to be aware of the perspectives of others. Moreover, students can learn the importance of secrets and when secrets are important to tell, and how trust is broken if they do share a secret that should not be told.

Start by performing a magic trick for the group of participants. Participants can discuss what they think about the magic trick. What happened? What did they see? What do they think happened?

What does the magician think happened? How do people (children, teenagers, adults) feel when they see magic? What do the participants in the group think and feel about magic?

Discuss with the group that they are going to be tested on their secret keeping abilities over the next weeks. The group can engage in a discussion about what is a secret that should be told versus a secret that should not be told. The group can discuss:

- What happens when a secret is told that should not be?

- What happens when you share too much? (*It's no longer magic!*)

- Give an example of a secret that should not be shared.

- What details need to be shared?

- In life, what details might you share? What might you not share? Why?

- When you share too much, how do you feel? How might others feel?

- What are the limits of what should be shared? When? In what relationships?

- How would you feel if it were your secret?

- How might others' perspective change? What about trust? Why is trust important?

This secret they are going to learn will not be one they need to share with others, because if they do, others' perspectives will change. Tell the students they are going to be gaining some magical knowledge to help them do the magic trick as they are going to be indoctrinated into the Magician's Code.

MAGICIAN'S CODE

Have the participants raise their right hands. Read the following to them, breaking every few words to have them repeat: "I do solemnly swear, to uphold the secrets of the Magician's Code, as I am about to learn about magical powers that make others feel happy, full of wonder, and surprise. I vow not to ruin the magical powers, for if I do, participants will no longer feel wonder and excitement about magic."

Next, the following steps can occur within a couple of sessions, but are best over time. Take one student aside and teach them how to do the magic trick before the next group meeting.

The student who knows the magic trick can present the magic trick to the class the next week. This student can help the group and teacher discuss their perspective before having the magical knowledge. Now that the student has the knowledge, discuss:

- How do they feel?

- Why is it important from the student's perspective to keep this knowledge to themselves? (*It would spoil the wonder and joy that others get from magic.*)

- What are the others' perspectives? How do they see the magic trick? What do they think happened?

- And is there a difference in perspective between the student who performed the magic trick and the rest of the group?

Another student can be trained to perform the magic trick, and the previous steps and discussion should be repeated. Once all of the group members know the magic trick, they will all be able to engage in a conversation about how their perspectives changed. Other discussion questions could include how they thought about the magic trick beforehand and what others who don't have the magic trick secret would think happened.

This will bring the group into a discussion on situations about which others may have different perspectives. Each group member can be encouraged to volunteer what their individual "preferred" perspective is—to know the magic trick, or to be an audience member and be amazed. Each perspective should be celebrated and group members can practice affirming others' differing perspectives.

Besides teaching magic perspectives, improv and acting in different personas are wonderful methods to increase perspective taking. When acting in a role, one is expected to dive into character, trying to become someone with a different perspective. In this improv game, the benefits are from utilizing one's observation skills to mirror another person and trying to figure out feelings, wants, and thoughts.

THE PUPPETEER IMPROV GAME

The Puppeteer is also a well-known and common theatre game in Gesell's book *Playing Along* (1997), which is utilized to mimic, read, and react to others' body language and expression. In The Puppeteer Improv Game, a groups of three is needed. One participant is the creator, another participant is the clay, and the other participant is the one who is trying to model the clay's feelings, actions, and facial expression. The puppet master pulls on imaginary strings on the puppet to shape the clay into a person, with a pose and expression. The participant who is mirroring the clay person tries to mirror exactly the facial and body expressions of the clay person. The person mirroring is then asked what it feels like to be the clay person. Gesell's (1997) recommended questions include: What do you know about the clay person? What is the clay person feeling? What are they thinking? What makes this person strong? What does the clay person want to do?

A challenge that can be added is to ask the person who is the model of the clay's feelings, to act out a persona of the clay. Then, have the clay, the sculptor, and the person acting out the persona discuss what matched the sculptor and clay's perspective of the clay character.

HELLO JELLO!

*Written by playwriting contest winner Jalina (4th grader)
along with help from three collaborating friends*

CHARACTERS

- √ Lizi—bully
- √ Crystal—victim
- √ Friends—Jessica (could add a couple more)
- √ Narrator—who is also a friend

At their lockers on stage left, the students are getting their books and materials ready.

Lizi: [*Walks up to Crystal and swings her around, causing Crystal to drop her books, stating in a sarcastic tone.*] Hey Hobo. Wanna come to my party?

Crystal: [*Looking surprised, confused, and uncomfortable... dramatic pause.*]

The students look uncomfortable, confused, and surprised also... dramatic pause.

> Crystal: [*Softly*] Um...okay.

> Jessica: Ugh... I like turtles and trains?

> Narrator: FREEZE!

> What happened here?

> What is Crystal feeling? What is Crystal thinking?

> What is Jessica feeling? What is Jessica thinking?

> Yes, that's right. Jessica is feeling uncomfortable. You can tell because she is not smiling, she is looking at Crystal who looks upset, AND she tries to change the subject.

> What is Lizi feeling? What is Lizi thinking?

> UNFREEZE!

The students leave with their books, and exit the stage. Lizi enters from stage right, preparing for the party. She sets up the party, makes sure the boombox is ready, pin the tail on the donkey is ready, and cups of juice and the prank cup of "jello" are ready.

Crystal and Jessica knock on the door and Lizi lets them in.

> Lizi: Welcome to my party! Does everyone want some juice? [*Lizi hands everyone a cup of juice (plastic cups colored with marker) and hands Crystal a cup with playdoh in it (jello).*]

The group stands together drinking their juice, and Crystal's "jello" (playdoh) falls out.

> Crystal: Eugh! Gross! This cup had jello in it, and now it's all over my face! LIZI! That's not funny!

> Jessica: Ummm... I like turtles and trains?

Crystal runs off the stage.

> Narrator: FREEZE!

> What is going on here?

What is Crystal feeling? What is Crystal thinking? What is Crystal's point of view?

What is Lizi feeling? What is Lizi thinking? What is Lizi's point of view?

What is Jessica feeling? What is Jessica thinking? What is Jessica's point of view?

What do you think might happen next?

UNFREEZE!

Lizi runs off stage and brings Crystal back to the party.

Lizi: Crystal, I am so sorry. I didn't know that would hurt your feelings. I was trying to be funny.

Crystal: Yeah, I did not like that. Please don't try to play a joke on me again.

Lizi: Okay, well...let's party!

Jessica turns on the music, the girls are dancing together, and Lizi decides to dance on a chair. The narrator asks Crystal if she wants to play pin the tail on the donkey. While blindfolded, Crystal accidentally pins the tail on Lizi's lower back.

Lizi: What is this? [*Laughs and pulls the tail off for everyone to see.*]

The girls laugh together and continue dancing. They get an idea, and go off stage, choosing one person each to come on stage and join the dance party. Each person gets a turn showing a dance move, while everyone else follows.

The leader or teacher can set up a screen with PowerPoint thought bubbles above each character, or have them hold thought bubbles above their heads.

Each character will be asked by the narrator what their perspectives are.

The characters will then share their thoughts, feelings, and perspectives. As required, the leader can guide the narrator's questions to get deeper answers.

Have the narrator or leader stand up in front of the characters of the play for the audience to ask questions. For more visuals, you can have thought bubbles projected or have the actors hold thought bubbles above their heads.

- Was this story about a conflict or a bullying situation?

- What is the difference between a bullying situation and a conflict?

- If you were Crystal, would you also forgive Lizi? Why?

It's important to recognize that Lizi apologized and admitted she was wrong. Crystal and Lizi are friends and Lizi thought she was funny, but agreed to stop her hurtful humor. It's not worth losing a friendship over a small problem, besides, if one small problem caused us to end a friendship, we would not have friends. In all relationships, there are conflicts—it's just about being able to talk it out.

Chapter Eight

PERFORMING WHEN ANXIOUS AND SHY... AND CLOWNING!!!!

As helpers, we have all worked with those who are anxious and shy. These individuals swear up and down they could never get in front of people. However, there are ways to get them involved without them even knowing about our plan for exposing them more to the idea of performing in order to lessen their fear of being in front of and/or around other people.

DECREASING PERFORMANCE STRESS LEVELS

When utilizing improvisational theatre, I have found Joseph Wolpe's method of "graduated exposure" helpful to motivate students and participants who are anxious about performing. Some students participate only during the script-writing process and do not want to be on stage. These students are typically wonderful observers, and are expected to watch the others perform the ideas and then give feedback. These participants are also encouraged to help getting props for us and helping to arrange items on stage. When feeling more comfortable, hesitant students are invited to join group improvisational games that we play on the floor in front of the stage. In order to increase their exposure to the stage, we will move the improvisational games onto the stage. Then, we transition into a part of a play that also mirrors as an improvisational game. One of these segments of our plays is the Slow Motion Snowball Fight. From there, we transition into practicing the play "7 Ways to Defeat a Bully." If participants feel uncomfortable at any point, they are allowed to sit and watch from the audience to give feedback.

However, in working with individuals who are anxious and shy, I have found that clowning is the most powerful tool. It has been my experience that children open up with laughter and expression within the first few minutes of learning a clown skit.

CLOWNING, A POWERFUL TOOL, WITH CAUTION

Be cautious of using the strategies in this chapter, as many participants might not be able to separate this type of stage behavior from real life social situations. We do not want them to actually use the behavior from the skits in this chapter!

As you know, Social Theatre™ morphed into comedy improv from its origins in a clowning program. These skits were collaboratively developed in my clown troupe program at Charles J. Sahs Elementary School between 2000 and 2012. I continue to use these skits with students during sessions and as ice breakers to help children feel more open with each other.

There is still incredible value in teaching clowning; it just has to be utilized correctly. I have utilized clowning for clients and students who are anxious and shy and have witnessed amazing results in as little as one session! I have seen students connect socially with others who have had difficulty in the general environment, and then began to feel more comfortable with peers. At other times, I have witnessed clowning help students with anxiety and extreme shyness begin talking when in costume, then generalizing to greater environments.

SETTING RULES FOR WHEN CLOWNING SHOULD AND SHOULD NOT BE USED

Set boundaries with the participants by explaining they should not actually use this type of behavior in social situations, rather only on stage when in the group. They are welcome to create silly skits and bring them to you, but not to try to recreate these types of behavior in social situations because others will feel it is strange. Thus, please utilize the skits from this chapter to help anxious and shy clients and/ or students to express themselves and increase confidence.

GRADUATED EXPOSURE AND CHARACTER DEVELOPMENT

If a participant is extremely anxious, utilize Joseph Wolpe's "graduated exposure" method. Have the participant dress in the clown clothes and start off stage with a skit or character that does not include talking. Once comfortable, the participant can practice on the stage, in front of someone, or be given a small talking part. Once given a small talking part and comfortable, increase the stimulus and expectations again by giving them a bigger talking part, asking them to go up on stage, or including more people to watch.

Characters who do not talk

- Both clowns in "Catch That Fly"

- Both clowns in "Leap Frog"

- The one who holds the popcorn in "Scary Movie"

- The sad clown in "Clown Surgery."

Characters who say one word

- First clown in "Hide and Seek"

- Clown who scares others in "Scary Movie."

Clown character development

When clowning, each participant is encouraged to develop their character.

1. What is the clown's name?

2. What is the clown's personality like? (e.g. bubbly, grouchy, clumsy, heroic, overconfident, etc.)

3. How does the clown move?

4. How does the clown talk? Or laugh?

5. What is the clown's purpose?

6. Is there a certain quirk the clown has?

Everything that a clown does must be a big production, with bigger and slower dramatic movements. The leader will have to do some modeling of what dramatically big and slow movement means. Having participants practice these skills is not only really fun, but also teaches self-control and expression! Some examples would be:

- When swinging a baseball bat, bend at the waist and stick out the rear end, hit the ground with the bat slowly, and slowly swing the bat.

- When chasing each other, clowns must run slowly and never catch each other, leaving at least 10 feet of space in between. Clowns run with a massive amount of facial expression as well as waving their arms in the air.

- When getting an idea, a clown must bend at their knees, point their finger, scoop their finger from their knees and jump while pointing their finger as far as they can up into the air and keeping it there for 2 seconds.

CATCH THAT FLY!

This scene takes place in a park. So the "clowns" have to make up a character who would be doing something in a park.

CHARACTERS

√ Clown sitting on a bench. Examples of characterizations for the clown on the bench are: person talking on the phone, person reading, person knitting, or person playing a game/ texting on their phone.

√ Clown who is trying to catch the fly. Examples of characterizations for this clown are a person trying to dramatically practice their baseball swing, playing an unsuccessful game of Frisbee golf, training to be a Tai Chi master, honing their karate moves, practicing meditation and yoga, or carrying a huge flower, smelling it, walking, and enjoying the sunshine.

One clown sits down on a bench, establishing the scene. They need to say something about being in the park on a nice day to let the audience know they are in a park. Once the clown establishes

the scene and their role while sitting on the bench, the other clown walks on to stage, looks around, and re-establishes the scene by making a comment about being in the park and wanting to do their activity of choice (see above). While the clown on the bench is doing their activity, and the clown who will catch the fly is practicing their activity they are not interacting with each other, which goes on for a minute or two. Into a microphone, someone from off stage makes a fly sound as the clown standing looks around in circles with their head as if they are trying to catch the fly. If this character has a prop such as a baseball bat or flower, they can use it to catch the fly, or they can just try to catch it with their hand or clap in the air.

As the clown is trying to catch the fly, the clown and the person off stage making the fly sound have to work together with their timing, paying attention to each other. The fly lands on the head of the clown who is sitting on the bench. The clown who is trying to catch the fly is only paying attention to the fly and not paying attention to the fact that the fly just landed on the other clown's head. The clown on the bench is oblivious to the fact that the clown trying to catch the fly is behind them. The clown trying to catch the fly pauses, looks at the fly, and takes their prop or hands and puts them up as high as they can. Slowly, the clown trying to catch the fly brings their arms down with the prop or without the prop and tries to swat the fly. If not using a prop, the clown can also make a big deal out of getting fly guts on themself as they squash it.

The clown on the bench makes a grouchy noise ("Hmph"), gets up slowly, turns around *slowly*, and puts their hands on their hips. Then the clown slowly, and in a big motion, points and shakes their finger at the other clown. Then the clown from the bench chases the other clown off stage with a clown run.

LEAP FROG

CHARACTERS

√ Clown who gets the idea to play leap frog
√ Clown who pulls a prank

The clowns start at opposite ends of the stage. The clowns walk toward each other, making eye contact, waving, and greeting each other. They stop, scratch/or tap their chins to show thinking, and one clown gets the idea to play leap frog. The clown who has the idea squats down while looking at the other clown and jumps like a frog. The other clown nods because they understand. Both clowns walk all the way to one side of the stage, one of the clowns squats down, and they play leap frog for two or three rounds. When the prankster clown stands up, they hold their finger to their lips, bend their knees, and smoothly move their body and head from the right side of the audience as they move to the middle and the left side of the audience while looking at them. The prankster clown is non-verbally telling them "Shhhh... I'm about to do something, don't tell!" The prankster clown takes their foot, pulls it back in a slow, big motion, then slowly and softly kicks the bottom of the other clown's shoe. The other clown reacts by making a dramatic slow leap and fall forward, or might even choose to do a forward roll.

The other clown, who had the idea to play leap frog, slowly stands up, puts their hands on their hips, and slowly and dramatically with big movements waves a finger at the prankster clown. The clown chases the prankster clown off stage.

HIDE AND SEEK

CHARACTERS

- √ First clown
- √ Second clown

The social advantage of this skit is also to practice seeing out of peripheral vision.

First clown: [*Tiptoes out on stage, looks to audience. Mimes and/ or says*] Shhhhh!!! [*Disappears behind a self-standing screen or room divider.*]

Second clown: [*Walks out on stage, looking around.*] Hmmmm... Have you seen my friend? We are supposed to play hide and seek.

Second clown listens to the audience, walking towards where they are pointing, avoiding looking at first clown, instead keeping first clown in peripheral vision.

First clown walks behind second clown, non-verbally making fun of second clown.

Second clown walks to opposite side of the screen, while first clown ducks and crawls in front of the screen so they are noticed. They go around one or two times.

First clown walks back behind the screen.

Second clown walks around the screen trying to find the other clown.

First clown: [*Pops out in front of the screen, yelling*] Boo!

Second clown chases first clown off the stage. Both run slow and dramatically, with their arms in the air.

SCARY MOVIE

Have participants engage in the Feeling or Action? and Voice Levels activities in Chapter Six before doing this skit. They will need to increase their scared feelings from 1 to 5 gradually in this skit, which adds to the buildup, climax, and hilarity of this skit.

CHARACTERS

- √ Prankster clown
- √ Scared clown who is trying not to show their fear
- √ Clown holding popcorn
- √ Clown holding remote

The clowns walk on stage, some sit on a bench and others on the floor, to create different stage levels.

Clown holding the remote: What do you guys want to watch?

Any or all of the clowns: A scary movie!

The clown holding the remote channel surfs, stopping on ridiculously non-scary shows such as *Dora the Explorer,*

SpongeBob SquarePants, or *Trolls,* or any movie/show that is popular at the time.

The clowns act like the shows are scary, by saying things like: "Ugh. Yeah. I don't want to watch Dora, she is TOO scary."

Then, the clowns decide on a non-scary show, such as *SpongeBob SquarePants.* They start at a low-level scared feeling of level 1, increasing their feelings collaboratively to a level 5 scared feeling.

They make comments such as: "Wow, that sponge is creepy, he is wearing pants!" "They eat at the Krusty Krab?! That sounds dangerous." "Squidward has tentacles! I'm really scared of tentacles!" "Oh my gosh! They are going to drown!"

As they are watching the movie and gradually working their way through scared feelings, the scared clown who is trying not to show their fear is shaking and acting even more scared than everyone else. However, the clown is trying to act not scared.

Scared clown: [*To the clown holding the popcorn.*] I'm not scared, are you scared? You are totally scared!

The clown holding the popcorn is scared too, but not as scared as the scared clown.

Prankster clown: [*Stands up.*] Guys, I'm going to get juice. You guys thirsty?

Once the clowns agree that they are thirsty, the prankster clown goes off stage. When the prankster clown brings the juice back, the prankster clown walks quietly and puts down the juice, tiptoeing, putting their finger over their mouth.

By now the other clowns are at the maximum level of scared from watching SpongeBob.

Prankster clown: [*Slowly and quietly stands behind the other clowns.*] BOO!

The clown with the popcorn flips the popcorn (a string of popcorn or Styrofoam peanuts) out of the bowl and the others jump out of their chairs or up from the floor in fear.

The clowns all chase the prankster clown off stage.

CLOWN SURGERY

CHARACTERS

√   Doctor
√   Sad clown patient
√   Assistant

PROPS (SOME CAN BE MIMED)

√   A BIG pair of clown scissors (can get at a dollar store)
√   A bone (can get at Halloween store or pet store)
√   A clipboard
√   Pair of clown pants
√   A colorful button-down shirt (polka dots work great too!)
√   Clown shoes (cheap, plastic ones from Halloween store)
√   Clown hat
√   Clown tie
√   Clown nose
√   Latex gloves
√   Toy hammer—the bigger the better!
√   Balloon pump
√   Big toothbrush
√   Loofah
√   Big bowl
√   Bench covered with material or sheet to hide props behind it.

The doctor and assistant walk on stage.

Doctor: Assistant! Prepare for surgery!

The assistant and doctor stand by a sink (bowl on table) and wash their hands. They also brush their teeth, and with the loofah, wash their face, their arms, and all the way up including their armpits. Afterward, they can dry their hands on their pants or shirt, then put their latex gloves on. As a clown everything is big, so in putting on the latex gloves, the movement needs to be big. When putting on the gloves, the arm needs to be extended high in the air in a dramatic fashion. For added humor, a glove can even be slingshot across the stage.

They are now done with preparing for surgery.

Doctor: Assistant! Bring in the patient!

The assistant responds and gets the patient from backstage. The patient is crying and cries all the way to the operating table (the bench).

Doctor: Assistant! Lie the patient on the table!

The assistant helps the patient lie on the table. The doctor talks to the patient and the doctor's bad breath knocks the patient out.

Doctor: Assistant! Scissors!

The assistant hands the doctor scissors, and the doctor pretends to cut the patient's stomach. At this point, creativity comes into play. Many things can be pulled out of a patient's stomach! We've used a rubber chicken and sausages, among other items. The last item to come out is the patient's *funny bone*.

The doctor holds the funny bone.

Doctor: Assistant! Tickle the funny bone!

The assistant tickles the funny bone.

Patient: HaHaHahahahahaha!

The doctor puts the funny bone back in (back behind the bench) and pretends to sew the patient back up.

Doctor: Assistant! Clown pants!

The assistant gives the doctor the pants and helps hold the patient's legs as the doctor puts on the pants. Some help from the patient is needed here as well. This is actually a good time for the patient to snore and/or sleep talk. Creative snores—such as Big Bird's snore from *Sesame Street*—are really funny!

Doctor: Assistant! Clown shirt!

Assistant: Doctor! We are losing him by 1000 degrees!

Doctor: [*Now in a big hurry!*] Assistant! Clown tie! Clown hat! Clown nose!

Assistant: Whew! That was close!

Doctor: Assistant! Clown shoes!

The assistant hands the shoes to the doctor and they are put on.

The doctor turns around to mark the patient's chart, the doctor's rear end facing the patient's clown shoes.

Doctor: Assistant! Test reflexes!

The assistant taps one knee with the hammer, the doctor gets kicked in the rear end. The assistant then reaches for the chart to write the result, bending at the waist waiting for the doctor to hit the other knee. The doctor takes the hammer, hits the patient's knee, and the clown shoe lightly kicks the assistant's face, making the assistant fall. The assistant gets up and then writes the results on the chart.

Doctor: Assistant! Laughing gas! [or can say "Assistant! Tickle!"]

The assistant gives the doctor the balloon pump and pumps air on the patient's face, making the patient laugh, and causing the patient to wake up.

Doctor: Surgery complete!

The assistant helps the patient get up and the assistant walks by the patient as the patient is incredibly animated and happy— even laughing hysterically as they walk off the stage.

As you can see, giving participants who are anxious and shy a platform to create fun together can be healing in many regards. Laughter, imaginative opportunities, stage interaction, and character development can help tear down walls of nervousness through silly stage communication! However, boundaries must also be set with those who might try to utilize this humor with others who are not part of the intervention and/or at the wrong times.

Chapter Nine

BEING CONFIDENT TO DEFEAT BULLYING

PRACTICING STYLES OF COMMUNICATION AND ASSERTIVENESS SKILLS

Alongside these skits, it is important to teach students the different styles of communication: passive, assertive, and aggressive. Breaking these communication patterns down into defining modalities of communication such as tone of voice, words, spatial relations, body stance, hands, facial expression, and eye gaze can teach students how to monitor themselves and recognize cues in others.

In chapter 17 of Desai's *A Rights-based Preventative Approach for Psychosocial Well-being in Childhood* (2010), assertiveness training methods are discussed. The styles of communication of "aggressive," "assertive," and "passive" are the concepts to be taught. Desai emphasizes teaching how each style of communication has different body language, tone of voice, and words.

In the following skits, these styles of communication are important, not only for being in character on stage, but also to help participants recognize the different styles of communication within themselves as well as others.

A specific example would be discussing how someone can demonstrate mixed messages by being passive with their voice (laughing while speaking, for example), but saying "stop" with assertive words at the same time. Further, they can learn how to match and increase awareness of styles of communication through practicing different roles. When rehearsing behaviors, participants can identify styles of communication within themselves as well as when others are exhibiting certain communication styles. In the following, participants will have opportunities to practice each style and process what it feels like in these roles.

When choosing which participants play which parts, those who mainly exert aggressive types of communication could play the victim roles, whereas those who are mainly passive in their communication styles could play the bully roles. I've found, especially for those who are typically passive and shy, these participants have shown more confidence and have actually gained some assertiveness skills through playing aggressive characters. For those who are typically aggressive communicators, they can see through the lens of someone who struggles with confidence and is picked on. This continued practice and characterization can also help develop empathy.

STYLES OF COMMUNICATION ACTIVITY

Goal: To have all modalities of communication be assertive, which is the ultimate demonstration of confidence.

In Appendix C, there are printable styles of communication cards labeled "Assertive," "Aggressive," and "Passive." These are the three styles of communication. The other cards are labeled "Body," "Hands," "Face," "Eyes," "Tone of Voice," and "Words." These cards are to be cut out, and the three styles of communication are to be placed on top—taped on a wall, placed on a board, or in a small group, placed on the table.

The group members can brainstorm a list of times people might have conflicts. A group participant then secretly chooses what style of communication to act out in response to the conflict. The others evaluate the participant's response according to whether their body language, words, and tone of voice match a style of communication category. The group then asks the participant if they were trying to act the way they identified. Then, the next participant can try a style of communication until all styles have been covered. Participants are guided through the process in having all modalities of communication match. The leader can demonstrate what it looks like when a facial expression does not match words being said. This can be a discussion point as participants can then understand how mixed signals occur. Moreover, if each participant is able to demonstrate strong examples of assertive, non-assertive, and aggressive communication, this will also be helpful in character development.

After doing this activity, reinforce with the participants that they are to utilize these skills to demonstrate who their characters are. When creating a play utilizing these personas, the goal will be to have the bystanders and victims become assertive by the end of the play.

"If You Want to be Cool" is a play written from the origins of Social Theatre™, our 2002 clown troupe. It is a play about peer pressure and how to just be yourself.

IF YOU WANT TO BE COOL

Written and performed by the Sahs Clown Troupe 2002, now Comedy Improv

CHARACTERS

√ Mattie—Leader
√ Angie, Payton, Brooklyn, Ada—followers
√ Ada—narrator
√ Charlie—left out

SCENE I

Charlie, standing alone by the wall. Looks sad because he does not have any friends.

Mattie: If you want to be cool, do this...

Walks silly, snapping fingers.

Mattie: If you want to be cool, you gotta do this...

Bops head up and down.

Mattie: If you want to be cool, you have to do this...

Raises his hands, wiggles fingers, wiggles hips.

All this time, the followers follow and do what is needed to be cool.

Charlie, feeling lonely, approaches the crowd.

Mattie: If you want to be cool, you gotta do this...

Jumps up and down.

Charlie, trying to fit in by jumping, trips and falls. Looks very sad and embarrassed.

SCENE II

Narrator: Freeze!

[*To the audience.*] What is going on with these kids?

What are they doing to act cool?

Should you have to do silly things to be cool?

What are things kids try to get you to do, in order to be cool? *(Be mean to others, start fights, spread rumors, drugs, drinking, etc.)*

What is Charlie doing to try to fit in?

What happened to him?

Do you think it's okay for him to just be himself?

What can he do to really be cool?

(Be nice, help others, say nice things, talk to others about what they like, set boundaries for how he wants to be treated.)

Is it okay for you to be yourself?

What might others do in this situation? Is there anything they can do to help Charlie?

Want to see what happens? Let's rewind this, okay.

Unfreeze!

Reverse!

The actors all go into reverse, as if a tape were rewinding, and resume their original positions.

SCENE III

Charlie, standing alone by the wall. Looks sad because he does not have any friends.

Mattie: If you want to be cool, do this...

Walks silly, snapping fingers.

Mattie: If you want to be cool, you gotta do this...

Bops head up and down.

Mattie: If you want to be cool, you have to do this...

Raises his hands, wiggles fingers, wiggles hips.

All this time, the followers follow and do what is needed to be cool.

Charlie, feeling lonely, approaches the crowd.

Mattie: If you want to be cool, you gotta do this...

Jumps up and down.

Charlie: [*Starts to jump, but then, gets an idea all of a sudden.*] Can I join your group?

Followers and Mattie: No, no way! You don't belong in our group! You are not cool!

Followers: [*Start thinking.*] Maybe we should let him be in our group. Yeah. Maybe he's cool. We won't really know if he's cool until we find out.

Charlie: Yeah, I don't have to do all that stuff, in order to be cool! You don't have to do that either!

Mattie: No! Don't listen to him. I don't want to be his friend and you shouldn't be his friend either.

Followers: Decide to be friends with Charlie and walk away from Mattie. Talking and laughing with Charlie when...

Mattie: [*Looks lonely by himself, decides to join this group.*] Hey, don't leave me! I'll join your group, just let me be your friend.

Charlie: You know what? We could just all be friends. We don't have to have silly rules, either. We can all be cool and be ourselves.

INVISIBLE GIRL

Written by Isabella, Chloe, Sylwia, and Brianna for Bully Prevention Week at Sahs School, February 2017 (parent permission obtained to publish)

CHARACTERS

- √ Girl—Ricky
- √ Student who gets chosen at PE—Diego
- √ Popular girl who sits with Ricky at lunch—Tracy (a little unconfident)
- √ Arnie Llama (bully)—captain of team A
- √ Hermione (bully follower)—captain of team B
- √ Angela (friend of Tracy)
- √ Angle (follower of Arnie Llama)
- √ Coach/lunch supervisor/outdoor supervisor/narrator

HERMIONE'S GROUP

- √ Diego
- √ Tracy

ARNIE LLAMA'S GROUP

- √ Angela
- √ Angle

SCENE I

Before school, Ricky tries to join the big group and approaches them.

Arnie Llama: You're annoying.

Angle: [*Agrees*] Yeah.

Other group members are silent...look uncomfortable.

Ricky then leaves the group and sits by herself in the corner.

Tracy: Be nice. She only wanted to hang around us.

Bell rings.

Exit stage.

SCENE II
Ricky appears sad and alone during gym class.

> Coach: Hermoine, you are captain, and Arnie Llama, you are captain. Pick your teams.

> Hermione: I pick Tracy and Angela.

> Arnie Llama: I pick Diego and Angle.

Awkward silence.

> Coach: You are forgetting one more person; whose team is she going on?

> Arnie Llama [*Whispers*] I'm not taking her, you take her.

> Hermione: [*Whispers*] I don't want her either.

> Tracy: [*To Hermoine*] Ridiculous. Let her join us.

> Arnie Llama: Rock, paper, scissors?

Arnie Llama and Hermione play rock, paper, scissors. Hermoine wins.

> Arnie Llama: Ricky, you are on the scoreboard.

The team then starts playing and Ricky watches by the scoreboard. Bell rings.

SCENE III
In the lunchroom, everyone is seated. Ricky gets her tray and tries to sit with the others, but they put their coats down. Ricky moves, sad, to the bleachers and eats by herself.

> Arnie Llama: That's so funny how she's trying to be all cool and she's not.

The others laugh and go along with Arnie Llama.

Ricky notices their mean body language, gestures, and eye gaze toward her.

> Tracy: You guys are mean. I'm going over there to sit with her.

> Arnie Llama: Yeah, whatever. You go...go be a loser with her.

Narrator: FREEZE!

What is going on?

How is Tracy feeling?

What might other kids be feeling?

What should the other kids do?

What might Ricky want to do?

(Maybe Ricky could look around to recognize who is nice.)

Unfreeze/rewind to beginning!

SCENE I
Ricky recognizes who is nice. Ricky goes to a different spot in the group. Tracy makes room for her in the circle and smiles at her.

Arnie Llama: Hey, Tracy! Why'd you let her in the group? She doesn't belong with us.

Tracy: She belongs with us, stop being a bully.

Bell rings.

SCENE II
Ricky appears sad and alone during gym class.

Coach: Hermoine, you are captain, and Arnie Llama, you are captain. Pick your teams.

Hermione: I pick Tracy and Angela.

Arnie Llama: I pick Diego and Angle.

Awkward silence.

Coach: You are forgetting one more person; whose team is she going on?

Arnie Llama [*Whispers*] I'm not taking her, you take her.

Hermione: [*Whispers*] I don't want her either.

Tracy: [Says to her team] No, Ricky is going to be on our team. Ricky, you just stand by me.

Another team member starts to agree and the majority wins. Ricky becomes part of the team.

SCENE III
In the lunchroom, everyone is seated. Ricky gets her tray and tries to sit with the others, but they put their coats down. Ricky moves, sad, to the bleachers and eats by herself.

> Arnie Llama: That's so funny how she's trying to be all cool and she's not.

> Tracy: You guys are mean. I'm going over there to sit with her.

One by one, each student stands up and tells Arnie Llama he is being mean and they are choosing to be with friends who are nice. Arnie Llama is left sitting by himself.

> Arnie Llama: Whatever, I don't care. I'll sit here by myself, but they'll come back!

The others are sitting together with Ricky and all talking together having fun.

The bell rings, the group gestures for Ricky to come with them. They walk off one side of the stage. Arnie Llama walks in the other direction, exits the stage, then runs back on the stage after the group—demonstrating that he does actually want to be part of the group.

After the play, process one more question: why did the group leave the bully?

7 WAYS TO DEFEAT A BULLY
Written by the Sahs Clown Troupe 2007, now Comedy Improv

CHARACTERS
- √ Bully
- √ Victim
- √ Narrator
- √ Friends
- √ Teacher

PROPS

✓   Big box marked "Send to China"
✓   Big bottle of glue
✓   Magic wand
✓   Song "Chariots of Fire" (Vangelis 1981)

The victim and bully are walking in the hallway. The victim is not paying attention and bumps into the bully.

Bully: HEY! Watch it, loser! [*Bully gets in victim's space and makes the motion to hit the victim.*]

Narrator: FREEZE!

What's going on here?

Who is the victim? Who is the bully?

What should they do?

The narrator takes answers and ideas from the audience on what the victim should do.

Narrator: Those are all GREAT ideas! But, let's try this first. [*Unfreezes the victim by tapping them on their shoulder.*]

Narrator: [*Loud talking but show whispering by putting hand by mouth while telling victim*] Here's some glue [*hands victim glue*], GLUE the bully to the floor!

Narrator: UNFREEZE!

The victim tries to pour glue around the bully's shoes, but the bully steps over the glue, gets in the victim's space, and makes a movement toward punching—without actually punching—the victim.

Narrator: FREEZE!

Well...that didn't work! Maybe putting glue on a bully is a bully type of behavior... What else would work?

The narrator takes answers and ideas from the audience on what the victim should do.

Narrator: Those are all GREAT ideas! But, let's try this first. [*Unfreezes the victim by tapping them on their shoulder.*]

Narrator: [*Loud talking but show whispering by putting hand by mouth while telling victim*] Here's a box [*hands victim box*], send the bully to China!

Narrator: UNFREEZE!

Bully: [*Holding hand up in a threatening way, in victim's space.*] What are you going to do now? Try me!

Victim: [*Puts box over bully's head.*] I'm going to send you to China!

The bully walks off stage with the box on their head.

The victim jumps up and down in celebration.

The bully walks back on stage, box on head, and pushes the box off their head.

Bully: I'm back! [*Gets in victim's space, and pretends they are going to punch the victim.*]

Narrator: FREEZE!

I guess China didn't want him. Maybe trying to get rid of a problem will not work. What else could work?

The narrator takes answers and ideas from the audience on what the victim should do.

Narrator: Those are all GREAT ideas! But, let's try this first. [*Unfreezes the victim by tapping them on their shoulder.*]

Why don't you try making the bully disappear? [*Hands the victim a magic wand.*]

Victim: [*Holds wand up.*] Abracadabra! Disappear, bully!

Bully: You WISH you could make me disappear! [*Still in victim's space, and makes a gesture to show they are going to push the victim.*]

Narrator: FREEZE!

Well. That didn't work either! It IS really hard to just make a problem disappear, isn't it? What else could work?

The narrator takes answers and ideas from the audience on what the victim should do.

Narrator: Those are all GREAT ideas! But, let's try this first. [*Unfreezes the victim by tapping them on their shoulder.*]

Why don't you try running away?

UNFREEZE!

Bully: You are going to get it. You will never make me disappear, never! [*Gets in the victim's space again, and the victim runs under the bully's legs. The bully jumps around, the victim runs underneath the bully's legs again, the narrator freezes the scene while the victim is under the bully's legs.*]

Narrator: FREEZE!

Hmm... Running away hasn't worked either. In fact, running away probably feels awkward. [*Dramatic pause, looking at bully and victim.*

What else could work?

The narrator takes answers and ideas from the audience on what the victim should do.

Narrator: Those are all GREAT ideas! But, let's try this first. [*Unfreezes the victim by tapping them on their shoulder.*]

Why don't you try hitting back? UNFREEZE!

Bully: [*Laughing*] You can't hit me!

The victim puts their forehead on the bully's outstretched hand, as the victim is bending at their waist and their arms flailing, trying to hit the bully.

The bully files their nails, looking bored, or talking on the phone.

Narrator: FREEZE!

That didn't work! Hitting back is not a solution, and can cause a cycle of revenge where no one wins. Besides, there is ALWAYS someone who is stronger. What else could work?

The narrator takes answers and ideas from the audience on what the victim should do.

Narrator: Those are all GREAT ideas! But, let's try this first. [*Unfreezes the victim by tapping them on their shoulder.*] Let's have a snowball fight!

The song "Chariots of Fire" plays in the background. The narrator waves all of the actors on stage and they take their places in a slow motion snowball fight, trying to defeat the bully. The bully eventually gets everyone down, pretends to tease them as they are down.

The music can be turned down as the snowball fight is concluding. All except the bully and victim walk off the stage.

The bully gets in the victim's space.

The victim looks scared, and bends backwards, trying to keep away from the bully.

Narrator: FREEZE!

So...all those things didn't work. Hmmm... We need to try something that will really help. Any ideas?

The narrator takes answers and ideas from the audience on what the victim should do.

Narrator: GREAT idea! We will try telling the teacher!

Narrator: [*Taps the victim on the shoulder.*] Tell the teacher. UNFREEZE!

Bully: I told you! Don't mess with me!

The victim turns away, and goes up to the teacher.

Victim: Ms. Teacher, I don't know what to do. He is being really mean and trying to hit me.

Teacher: [*Faces the bully.*] We are not allowed to bully in this school. I will give you the opportunity to rethink your behavior in afterschool detention throughout this week.

Bully: Okay.

Teacher: I will also call your parents to let them know how you are doing.

Bully: PLEASE, PLEASE don't call my parents! I promise I'll never ever bully again!

Teacher: Come with me, we will talk about this further in afterschool detention.

The bully and the teacher walk off the stage.

YOU, ME, AND INDIVIDUALITY

Written by Brooke Gawel (in 6th grade), Safe Schools Week Playwriting contest winner of 2009 (permission obtained to use name and play)

CHARACTERS

√ Mark—boy with glasses
√ Ali—girl with hearing aids
√ Deanna—bully
√ Nikki—bystander
√ Narrator/teacher (and writer)

PROPS

√ Bluetooth earpiece
√ Glasses
√ Identical shirts or outfits to demonstrate sameness—wear on top of other clothes for the entire play
√ Different, colorful outfits and accessories to demonstrate uniqueness (tutus, feather boas, sunglasses, stick-on mustaches, baseball hats, headphones around neck, etc.)

SCENE I
The students are backstage, and the teacher is writing on the board getting ready for class. The bell rings. The students walk in and sit down.

Teacher: I will start as soon as everyone's ready for Math.

The students sit in their chairs. While the teacher is writing a problem on the board...

Deanna: Mark, why do you wear those DUMB glasses? You would look so much better without them.

Mark: Oh... [*Hesitantly removes his glasses.*]

Teacher: Ali, come up here and do this problem.

Ali takes her time, thinks, and writes the correct answer on the board.

Teacher: Great job, Ali.

Teacher: Deanna, your turn. This is your problem.

Teacher points to the board.

Deanna: Teacher, it's not my problem. [*Takes a writing utensil, writes smiley face on the board, puts the writing utensil back on the board, and sits down.*]

Teacher: Nikki, it's your turn.

Nikki stands up quickly, and walks to the board with an aura of overconfidence. Nikki figures out the problem quickly, writes the correct answer and turns toward the teacher, class, and audience, and announces confidently. The answer is _____.

Teacher: Good job, Nikki. Mark, it's your turn.

Mark: [*Bumps into things walking up to the board. He puts his nose up to the board, turns to the teacher.*] Eight.

As the teacher stands puzzled, the bell rings. The students grab their lunch and file out of the classroom, into the hallway. (The hallway is shown as the stage in front of the closed curtain.)

Deanna: Mark, since you don't have glasses any more, you are cool. You can totally hang with us now!

Nikki: Yeah, those glasses definitely were NOT cool.

Ali approaches the group.

Ali: Hey guys!

Deanna: Um...hi. What are those things in your ears?

Ali: They are my hearing aids, they help me hear.

Deanna: Yeah, the hearing aids...are NOT cool.

Ali: Okay, I'll just take them out. [*Takes out her hearing aids.*]

The group walks together as Mark feels his way around, and eventually runs into the wall or something else in his way.

The group exits the stage.

SCENE II
The group enters the stage, which is the cafeteria. Nikki, Deanna, and Mark sit down together.

Narrator: As the group sits together in the cafeteria...

Nikki: Let's split some pizza.

Deanna: Good idea.

Mark looks closely at his lunch and at the pizza.

Ali: [*Yelling loudly*] Hi guys!

Deanna, Mark, and Nikki: Hi!

Deanna: Want to sit with us and eat pizza?

Ali: [*Yelling loudly*] What? Eat PEAS?!

Deanna: Not peas, pizza!

Ali: Eugh! I hate PEAS!

Nikki writes PIZZA on a napkin. Holds it up.

Ali: Oh! Pizza! Of course! Thanks! [*Sits down and joins the group.*]

All finish lunch. The bell rings. The students leave the stage. The narrator walks on stage.

Narrator: Every day the students were trying to act cool just to impress others. The students, one by one, lost their individuality. Then, life became boring.

The students walk on stage wearing the same outfits and walking in the same pattern like robots, walking off the other side of the stage.

(The narrator can be creative here and add their own ideas about how being the same would make life boring.)

As the students are backstage, they have unique, colorful outfits on underneath their identical outfits (we used inside-out PE shirts) to reveal their uniqueness. Some wear feather boas and tutus, while others prefer baseball caps, etc. After changing to "uniqueness" the students walk back on stage—with different characterizations, and ways of walking. And, of course, Ali and Mark wear their hearing aids, and glasses.

Narrator: So, we all decided to be ourselves and live life as we accept and celebrate You, Me, and Individuality!

Chapter Ten

SOCIAL THEATRE™
HOW CAN I USE IT?

Social Theatre™ can be utilized in different ways, from use with individuals, small groups, in classrooms, in clinical settings, and entire schools or larger communities. The use of these different ways can also be coordinated together in a way that can create an invigorating cycle within the entire community. The following shows ways Social Theatre™ can be utilized in different settings.

SCHOOL-WIDE AND IN THE COMMUNITY
Playwriting contest

A school-wide or community-wide playwriting contest about a specific theme such as "Safe Schools," "Safe Communities," or other anti-bullying themes. Social Theatre™ group participants can also be active in looking at anonymous scripts to identify what they like about skits, to help in decision making for the winner.

Once a playwriting contest winner is chosen, that person can be contacted to help identify group members to help collaborate during the script re-writing process and for performing. If the playwriting contest winner does not have enough people, Social Theatre™ participants can also be invited to fill needed spots.

See Figure 10.1 on how playwriting contests can complement the Social Theatre™ group writing and performance cycle with regard to recruitment and increasing belongingness.

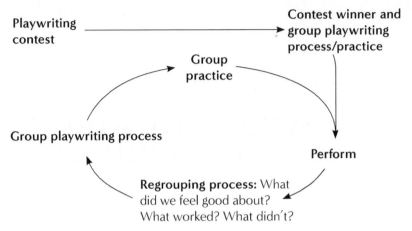

Figure 10.1 Playwriting and performance cycle of recruitment
Source: Author

Playwriting contest recruitment into Social Theatre™ program

At the end of each semester, include participants from the afterschool program and any playwriting contests together for a *performance*. Performances can be planned for different places in the community such as nursing homes, park district, school-wide assemblies, or classrooms. Ideal audiences would be for programs for others who could benefit from learning about social skills. Our favorite populations to perform for include those with cognitive disabilities, the elderly, and children who are younger than the performers. School assemblies, classrooms, special recreation programs, senior centers, and nursing homes are typically positive and accepting environments to perform in.

IN CLASSROOMS AND COMMUNITY PROGRAMS

Playwriting process

The playwriting process can be utilized in language arts or in community group programs and the skits could be performed for other classes/groups or in the community.

Role-plays

Utilize small groups or students from the class to perform plays or activities from this book to teach specific social and/or emotional concepts. Advantageously, Social Theatre™ participants are always ready to be pulled in front of the class as they are exposed to acting and have rehearsed skits and skills many times.

IN GROUP THERAPY, CLINICAL SETTINGS
In a clinical setting, Social Theatre™ finds that grouping to social-cognitive level is the most productive way to help participants learn. See Chapter Two, where it discusses the Social Thinking® Social Communication Profile (Winner, Crooke, and Madrigal n.d.; Socialthinking.com).

Improvisational activities
In the therapeutic setting, it is much more feasible to plan for participant needs when grouping by social-cognitive level. When planning improv activities, follow the improv activities for the social-cognitive level of your group participants, starting with the basic activities, and build challenges as listed under the activities, and as ability allows.

Playwriting process
Utilize the playwriting process as a tool to teach collaborative skills.

Empowering clients
Obtain consent to keep and/or share the skits with others to increase participants' feeling of importance that they are sharing their lessons about social skills, which can teach others. As the skits should be a collaboration of fictitious ideas, utilize them with the other groups and encourage clients to share their skits.

PERFORMANCE AND CONFIDENTIALITY
Depending on setting and type of therapy, some may be limited due to confidentiality laws. If this is the case, a performance can be set up for the groups' parents and, if consent to share ideas is obtained, the participants can share their skits with others such as their schools, etc. If a participant or parent does not want to participate in the performance, it is always their choice.

In my private practice, we have been able to have performances in smaller, more controlled settings, such as nursing homes, and for special recreation programs, as long as consent is obtained.

In following the *Illinois Mental Health and Developmental Disabilities Confidentiality Act* or the most stringent confidentiality law in your state or area, performance could be a possibility if you can gain consent from participants and their parents with the name of the place you are performing on the consent form. The possible consequences of performing in a small public setting should be discussed with parents and participants, such as the likelihood of seeing someone they know. However, parents and participants usually agree that the benefits of performance outweigh any risks. Besides, Social Theatre™ does not feel like therapy, especially when performing. In fact, I believe that performance is the most important part of the therapeutic process. Moreover, when we set up a performance, we call it "Social Theatre™" and do not disclose the nature of our group. The following is the way I always introduce my group.

> Community performance introduction: The youth of today get too wrapped up in their social media, their phones, their video games, and other devices as a way to socialize. This group of youngsters sees the importance of writing and performing skits about life lessons because they feel it is important to keep the face-to-face interaction, and this is why they write and perform these humorous plays about social skills.

After a performance, you will find that there is a lot of excitement and pride, which is a great place to expand on emotional growth!

A sidenote: With regard to insurance considerations, I do not charge for insurance for a public performance; rather, I charge parents a rate that is discussed with them and write a group information sheet.

IN SMALLER, NON-CLINICAL GROUPS
Collaborative writing process
In smaller classrooms, such as special education classes or other intervention type of groups, the collaborative playwriting process can be utilized.

Character development and writing
Participants can be given assignments to write from the perspective of each character, as well as describing the plot, the conflict, and resolution.

Performance

Once the class has been able to move through the Social Theatre™ playwriting process, the group can then perform their skit for a chosen audience.

WITH INDIVIDUALS IN EDUCATIONAL OR COMMUNITY SETTINGS

With individuals, pictures and videos of Social Theatre™ participants (from an educational or community-based program) that demonstrate social emotional concepts can be utilized. Depending on the setting, parent permission may be needed to utilize the pictures and video, but it is a powerful opportunity for role modeling and for positive student involvement. Oftentimes, this is an opportunity for others to connect to those who are familiar to them and they are then more motivated to learn.

Playwriting process

Individuals might also be interested in writing skits and brainstorming ideas that can be taken to the groups to utilize as a basis for brainstorming, or even a play. The individual can be introduced to the idea that their play will also go through a revision process—that not all the puzzle pieces fit. This is a cyclical process, as the individual writes a script, then other participants become part of the process to make the skit even better. These chosen participants also help perform the skit. Oftentimes, these individuals then feel more comfortable and are motivated to join Social Theatre™.

APPENDICES ▋

APPENDIX A
Common Core Standards, Social/Emotional Learning (SEL) Standards and Social Theatre™

Social Theatre™ fulfills many Common Core Standards (NGA and CCSSO 2010) under the area of Language Arts and Literature. Moreover, social emotional learning standards are also met by Social Theatre™. The unique aspect of Social Theatre™ is if a specific skill needs to be worked on more, the group can write a skit about this specific skill as they dissect the issue and how to resolve it. Those who struggle with the skill do not typically feel uncomfortable talking about their struggle as it is discussed in the third person, as a way to develop a skit to teach others.

Common Core Standards
Key ideas and details

Standard R.CCR.2 Determine central ideas or themes of a text and analyze their development; summarize the key supporting details and ideas.

> In Social Theatre™, students must identify the main idea of what lesson is being taught in the specific skit and discuss how to demonstrate the main idea without getting too much off track. The supporting details and ideas are the location, the characters' feelings, and characters' relationships with each other.

Standard R.CCR.3 Analyze how and why individuals, events, and ideas develop and interact over the course of a text.

During script development, participants must think of how and why individuals interact over the course of the skits. Thus, participants help brainstorm to build the conflict in the story, which reflects what they want to teach in their main idea.

Craft and structure

Standard R.CCR.6 Assess how point of view of purpose shaped the content and style of a text.

Understanding point of view is a theme in the Social Theatre™ program. In character development, participants collaborate on a character's personality and point of view, which contributes to the conflict and main idea in the story.

Integration of knowledge and ideas

Standard R.CCR.7 Integrate and evaluate content presented in diverse media and formats, including visually and quantitatively, as well as in words.

In Social Theatre™, participants are not forced but encouraged to keep their ideas written or drawn in a journal. These ideas are utilized in relation to others' ideas, which make up the skits the group writes. Participants are encouraged to bring in their own skits that reflect the ideas they have collected, as well as ideas brainstormed in group.

Standard R.CCR.8 Delineate and evaluate the argument and specific claims in a text, including the validity of the reasoning as well as the relevance and sufficiency of the evidence.

Once the main idea and conflict are decided, parts of the skit are practiced on stage. After practicing a segment, the group gets together to process how the ideas can merge together. As part of the collaborative writing process, the group analyzes their script to ensure the main idea, the conflict, and resolution all give enough detail for the audience to understand through the actual script text as well as the on stage non-verbal communication. Furthermore, the group members analyze the details of their script with regard to whether or not it reflects what they want the audience to learn and understand.

Text type and purposes

Standard W.CCR.3 Write narratives to develop real or imagined experiences or events using effective technique, well-chosen details, and well-structured event sequences.

Participants are encouraged to write narratives into a script, in order to support the events in the skit. The skits are intended to be simple, but written narratives add to characterizations and help shape the events in the skits.

Standard W.CCR.5 Develop and strengthen writing as needed by planning, revising, editing, re-writing, or trying a new approach.

One of the main components of Social Theatre™ is to brainstorm, write, practice, revise, and rewrite our plays and sketches.

Standard W.CCR.6 Use technology, including the internet, to produce and publish writing and to interact and collaborate with others.

In order to bring our sketches and plays together, students and the group leader utilize shared Google documents to view the current writings and can leave comments for collaboration. This helps with maintaining the flow of the editing process through to the next meeting.

Comprehension and collaboration

Standard SL.CCR.1 Prepare for and participate effectively in a range of conversations and collaborations with diverse partners, building on others' ideas and expressing their own clearly and persuasively.

In the Social Theatre™'s script-writing process, collaboration is key throughout the brainstorming process, writing, revising, and performing. The process includes teaching participants how to not only accept others' ideas, but be excited about others' ideas, and build on them.

Standard SL.CCR.3 Evaluate a speaker's point of view, reasoning, and use of evidence and rhetoric.

When establishing a character in a skit, the points of view are discussed. Each participant is also expected to learn and practice most of the roles, which provides a deeper understanding of each character's perspective. Moreover, participants are expected to learn all parts of the skit in order to boost understanding of points of view and reasoning behind it.

Collaborative for Academic, Social and Emotional Learning (CASEL)

CASEL, is a "Collaborative for Academic, Social, and Emotional Learning" which provides the guidelines for states to incorporate Social Emotional Learning into their plans for the Every Student Succeeds Act. The goal of CASEL is to advocate for evidence based Social and Emotional Learning to be equally integrated education for students from pre-school to high school across the United States (CASEL.org).

The Following Five CASEL Competencies are addressed in accordance with Social Theatre™.

Self-awareness

- **Identifying emotions**—In using theatre and improv games, recognizing and expressing emotions is practiced with almost every interaction.

- **Accurate self-perception**—In utilizing theatre, participants participate in self-discovery through character development. In Social Theatre™, pictures and video modeling can be utilized during improv, as a way to help participants see their communication and social skills in a more accurate light.

- **Recognizing strengths**—After performing, group members can sit down together to discuss strengths that they contributed.

- **Self-confidence**—Through many successful outlets, participants find confidence through sharing ideas, communicating and playing with others, group writing and performing.

- **Self-efficacy**—Being part of a collaborative process, participants learn they can be successful and they do have important contributions and ideas.

Self-management

- **Impulse control**—In working together to share the spotlight, impulse control is practiced. Many skits and activities have also been created, which addresses impulse control through slowed movement, turn taking, and social cue recognition.

- **Stress management**—Research shows that humor has been one of the most effective "buffers" between depression and functionality. In Social Theatre™, humor is utilized to make fun of social mishaps, as everyone has made social, emotional, and behavioral mistakes. We make humor out of mistakes, but then take time to recognize how others might feel in these situations, because we can only learn and do better. In the second part of our skits, we correct mistakes by incorporating strategies needed.

- **Self-discipline**—Through practicing how to overcome social and emotional mistakes, we practice strategies that demonstrate self-discipline and choices. When participants practice skits that utilize a strategy to make choices, they can more easily incorporate these strategies into life.

- **Self-motivation**—Participants feel successful in the group, due to the rule of all ideas being accepted. Participants will sometimes even volunteer to write scripts and keep an idea journal.

- **Goal-setting**—In smaller groups, participants can set a personal social, emotional, or behavioral goal to work on while participating in Social Theatre™.

- **Organizational skills**—Participants can attend to the idea book (or online document) as the Post-it® notes with ideas on them need to be grouped and placed on the correct pages.

Social awareness

- **Perspective-taking**—In character development and other strategies of Social Theatre™, perspective taking is addressed through interactive activities such as learning magic tricks, improv games, and already scripted skits.

- **Empathy**—In Social Theatre™, empathy is developed through group bonds, being able to play, develop, and understand characterizations that are different from oneself, and helping each other out while on stage.

- **Appreciating diversity**—Social Theatre™ has scripted plays about diverse populations (such as those with different abilities) and about having respect for each other.

- **Respect for others**—During the script development process, group participants go through a process that promotes respect and acceptance of all ideas. Moreover, the scripts that are written are about social skills and other social emotional lessons such as having empathy, respecting others, understanding perspective, and celebrating differences.

Relationship skills

- **Communication**—Using Social Theatre™, participants increase spontaneity and comfort in communication with others through opportunities in skits, and learning how to communicate ideas by being in the moment of improvisation.

- **Social engagement**—Improv activities focus on joint attention and mutual eye gaze. Activities and skits also give examples of appropriate and inappropriate reactions. Activities and skits also focus on conversation skills, how to initiate an invitation, recognize/match the environmental mood and activity, and how to recognize an accident or something done on purpose.

- **Relationship-building**—Participants build positive relationships as they are guided through a collaborative process together. Moreover, they learn skills on how to build relationships through their learning and practicing social skills through improv activities. Both improv and brainstorming focus on idea acceptance, but participants also learn to be flexible with their own and others' ideas.

- **Teamwork**—Group members collaborate through the process of script development, then have an option to perform their plays. In practice and performance, teamwork skills are practiced in order to achieve the goals of playwriting and completing fun activities.

Responsible decision making

- **Identifying problems**—In brainstorming, group members are asked to brainstorm what kids their age need to work on. The brainstorming process is essentially "free association" and group members do typically share about problems at this stage.

- **Analyzing situations**—Social Theatre™ activities and skits have participants define and dissect situations by practicing certain aspects. In "Big Problem, Little Problem," participants identify situations and reactions and identify which reactions are too small, too big, or appropriate. In the play development process, group participants are involved in analyzing problems through character development, practicing problems, and then solutions to see what works and what does not work.

- **Solving problems**—In the process of evaluating each other's ideas, possible solutions are practiced. In solving problems together collaboratively, group members come to the realization that sometimes their ideas may or may not fit into the skit. Through the group process, group members typically come to understand that ideas are puzzle pieces, and even if their idea did not make it into a skit, their ideas can be saved for the next skit.

- **Evaluating**—Group members are guided through the process of giving constructive, positive feedback of which ideas work and which ideas could make skits even better.

- **Reflecting**—After performing a skit, the group should reflect, discussing their best moments and what could be done even better next time. Group members should also discuss what they learned and what they would like to learn.

- **Ethical responsibility**—Social Theatre™'s goal is to write and perform skits that teach social skills lessons, and being a responsible participant is essential. Participants understand that their role is important as they are role models to those they are teaching skills to.

APPENDIX B
Feeling or Action?

Jumping	Throwing	Sad	Ambivalent
Cheering	Clapping	Mad	Happy
Kicking	Stretching	Surprised	Nervous
Pencil tapping	Dancing	Disgust	Bored
Painting	Swimming	Tired	Calm

APPENDIX C
Styles of communication
Cut into cards; it is helpful if you have a magnetic board with magnets on the back to move the cards around...or just using tape will work too.

Passive	Assertive	Aggressive
Hands	Tone of Voice	Face
Body	Words	Eyes

REFERENCES

Adams, P. and Mylander, M. (1998) *Gesundheit! Bringing good health to you, the medical system, and society through physician service, complementary therapies, humor and joy.* Rochester, Vermont: Healing Arts Press.

Adams, P. and Van Amerongen, J. (1998) *House Calls.* San Francisco, CA: Robert D. Reed Publishers.

Agnihotri, S., Gray, J., Colantonio, A., Polatajko, H., Cameron, D., Wiseman-Hakes, C., *et al.* (2012) 'Case report: Two case study evaluations of an arts-based social skills intervention for adolescents with childhood brain disorder.' *Developmental Neurorehabilitation 15*, 4, 284–297.

Aristotle (1981) *Aristotle's Metaphysics.* Trans. W.D. Ross. Oxford: Clarendon Press.

Baker, J.E. (2003) *Social Skills Training: For Children and Adolescents with Asperger Syndrome and Social-Communication Problems.* Shawnee Mission, KS: Autism Asperger Publishing Company.

Bandura, A. (1969) *The Principles of Behavior Modification.* New York: Holt, Rinehart and Winston.

Baron-Cohen, S. (1989) 'The autistic child's theory of mind: A case of specific developmental delay.' *The Journal of Child Psychology and Psychiatry 30*, 2, 285–297.

Bereiter, C. and Scardamalia, M. (1987) *The Psychology of Written Composition.* Hillsdale, NJ: Lawrence Erlbaum Associates.

Berk, L.S., Tan, S.A., Fry, W.F., Napier, B.J., Lee, J.W., Hubbard, R.W., Lewis, J.E., Eby, W.C. (1989) 'Neuroendocrine and Stress Hormone Changes During Mirthful Laughter.' *American Journal of the Medical Sciences 298*, 6, 390–396.

Boven, L.V., Loewenstein, G., Dunning, D., and Lordgren, L.F. (2013) 'Changing places: A dual judgment model of empathy gaps in emotional perspective taking.' *Advances in Experimental Social Psychology 48*, 117–171.

Buchanan, M. (n.d.) 'Improvs and Warmups.' Childdrama.com. Accessed on 4/28/2017 at www.childdrama.com/warmups.html

Burns, D.D. (1989) *The Feeling Good Handbook: Using the New Mood Therapy in Everyday Life.* New York: W. Morrow.

Centerstage (n.d.) *Teaching Playwriting in Schools: Teacher's Handbook.* Baltimore, MD: Centerstage. Retrieved on 4/17/2017 from www.learningtogive.org/sites/default/files/06playwrightshandbook.pdf

Chasen, L. (2011) *Social Skills, Emotional Growth and Drama Therapy: Inspiring Connection on the Autism Spectrum.* London: Jessica Kingsley Publishers.

Cohen, R. (2011) *Working Together in Theatre: Collaboration and Leadership.* New York: Palgrave Macmillan.

Collaborative for Academic, Social, and Emotional Learning (CASEL) (2017) *CORE SEL Competencies.* Accessed on 1/10/2017 at www.casel.org/core-competencies

Corbett, B.A., Gunther, J.R., Comins, D., Price, J., Ryan, N., Simon, D., Schupp, C.W., and Rios, T. (2011) 'Brief report: Theatre as therapy for children with autism spectrum disorder.' *Journal of Autism and Developmental Disorders 41*, 4, 505–511.

Corbett, B.A., Qualls, L.R., Valencia, B., Fecteau, S.M., and Swain, D.M. (2014a) 'Peer-mediated theatrical engagement for improving reciprocal social interaction in autism spectrum disorder.' *Frontiers in Pediatrics 2*, 110.

Corbett, B.A., Swain, D.M., Coke, C., Simon, D., Newsom, S., Houchins-Juarez, N. *et al.* (2014b) 'Improvement in social deficits in Autism Spectrum Disorders using a theatre-based, peer-mediated intervention.' *Autism Research 7*, 1, 4–16.

DeMichele, M. (2015) 'Improv and ink: Increasing individual writing fluency with collaborative improv.' *International Journal of Education and the Arts 16*, 10, 1–25.

Desai, M. (2010) *A Rights-based Preventative Approach for Psychosocial Well-being in Childhood.* Springer Science+Business Media B.V.

Energy Arts (n.d.) 'What is Chi?' Retrieved on 7/1/2017 from www.energyarts.com/what-is-chi

Frozen OST (2013) 'Do You Want To Build a Snowman?' Retrieved on 7/3/2017 from https://youtu.be/9MPGyx7N1XI?list=PLYvbP-7o5NQYF2u8URnzP8GX67kAHTRFX

Gesell, I. (1997) *Playing Along: 37 Group Learning Activities Borrowed from Improvisational Theatre.* Duluth, MN: Whole Person Associates.

Gillies, R.M. (2015) 'Developments in Collaborative Learning.' *Collaborative Learning: Developments in Research and Practice* (pp. 1–25). New York: Nova Science Publishers, Inc.

Gokhale, A.A. (1995) 'Collaborative learning enhances critical thinking.' *Journal of Technology Education 7*, 1, 22–30.

Guli, L.A., Semrud-Clikeman, M., Lerner, M.D., and Britton, N. (2013) 'Social Competence Intervention Program (SCIP): A pilot study of a creative drama program for youth with social difficulties.' *The Arts in Psychotherapy 40*, 37–44.

Hsing, C. (2015) *Visual Imagery Perspective and Conceptual Processing of Core Affect.* Electronic thesis. Retrieved on 7/03/2017 from https://etd.ohiolink.edu

Inside Out Deleted Scenes: Cast's Favourite (2015) Retrieved on 7/3/2017 from https://youtu.be/pFbID9f5UZw

Kamei, T. and Hiroaki, K. (1997) 'Changes of Immunoregulatory Cells Associated with Psychological Stress and Humor.' *Perceptual and Motor Skills 84*, 3, 1296–1298.

Kuiper, N.A., Martin, R.A. and Olinger, L.J. (1993). 'Coping humour, stress, and cognitive appraisals.' *Canadian Journal of Behavioural Science/Revue Canadienne des Sciences du Comportement 25*, 1, 81–96.

Kolb, D.A. (1984) *Experiential Learning: Experience as the Source of Learning and Development.* Englewood Cliffs, NJ: Prentice-Hall.

Kuypers, L.M. (2011) *The Zones of Regulation®: A Curriculum Designed to Foster Self-regulation and Emotional Control.* San Jose, CA: Think Social Publishing, Inc.

Le Clic (1995) "Call Me." *Tonight is the Night.* CD Soundtrack Single. New York: RCA.

Levinson, S.C. and Torreira, F. (2015) 'Timing in turn-taking and its implications for processing models of language.' *Frontiers in Psychology 6*, 731.

Linker, J. (2010, April 20) 'The 10 Commandments of Brainstorming.' Accessed 4/17/2017 from www.forbes.com/2010/04/20/brainstorming-ideation-ideas-leadership-managing-innovation.html

Mundy, P. (2016) *Autism and Joint Attention: Development, Neuroscience, and Clinical Fundamentals.* New York: The Guilford Press.

NGA (National Governors Association) and CCSSO (Council of Chief State School Officers) (2010) *Common Core State Standards English Language Arts.* Washington, DC: NGA Center for Best Practices.

Peterson, K., DeKato, L., and Kolb, D. (2015) 'Moving and learning: Expanding style and increasing flexibility.' *Journal of Experimental Education 38*, 3, 228–244.

Piaget, J. (1972) 'The mental development of the child.' In I.B. Weiner and D. Elkind (eds) *Readings in Child Development* (pp. 271–279). New York: John Wiley & Sons.

Plato (1989) *Plato: The Republic and Other Works.* Trans. B. Jowett. New York: Anchor Books.

Premack, D. and Woodruff, G. (1978) 'Does the chimpanzee have a theory of mind?' *Behavioral and Brain Sciences 4*, 4, 515–629.

Randolph, B. and Rich, S. (1963) 'Yakety Sax.' CD Soundtrack Single. Washington, DC: Monument Records.

Scott, W.A. (1962) 'Cognitive complexity and cognitive flexibility.' *American Sociological Association 25*, 405–414.

Seih, Y., Chung, C., and Pennebaker, J. (2011) 'Brief report: Experimental manipulations of perspective taking and perspective switching in expressive writing.' *Cognition and Emotion 25*, 5, 926–938.

Slama, H., Mary, A., Massat, I., and Pelgneux, P. (2011) 'Theory of mind and ADHD.' *ADHD in Practice 3*, 4.

Vangelis (1981) "Chariots of Fire." On single album *Chariots of Fire*. CD Soundtrack Film Score. London: Polydor Records.

Vass, E., Littleton, K., Miell, D., and Jones, A. (2008) 'The discourse of collaborative creative writing: Peer collaboration as a context for mutual inspiration.' *Thinking Skills and Creativity 3*, 192–202.

Vera, E.M., Vacek, K., Blackmon, S., Coyle, L., Gomez, K., Jorgenson, K. *et al.* (2012) 'Subjective wellbeing in urban, ethnically diverse adolescents: The role of stress and coping.' *Youth & Society 44*, 3, 331–347.

Winner, M.G. (2007) *Thinking About You, Thinking About Me*. San Jose, CA: Think Social Publishing, Inc.

Winner, M.G. (2013) *Why Teach Social Thinking®? Questioning Our Assumptions About What It Means to Learn Social Skills*. San Jose, CA: Think Social Publishing, Inc.

Winner, M.G. and Crooke, P. (2008) *You Are a Social Detective*. San Jose, CA: Think Social Publishing, Inc.

Winner, M.G. and Madrigal, S. (2013) *Superflex Takes on One-Sided Sid, Un-Wonderer and the Team of Unthinkables*. San Jose, CA: Think Social Publishing.

Winner, M.G. and Murphy, L. (2016) *Social Thinking® and Me* (two book set). San Jose, CA: Think Social Publishing, Inc.

Winner, M., Crooke, P. and Madrigal, S. (n.d.) 'The Social Thinking–Social Communication Profile™—Levels of the Social Mind.' Retrieved on 9/5/2017 from www.socialthinking.com/Articles?name=Social%20 Thinking%20Social%20Communication%20Profile

INDEX